Progress Plain and Si

CW00552543

What is progress in learning? How do we see progress being made in a lesson? This book offers a fresh perspective on teaching, learning and progress in the classroom. Written by an experienced teacher and school leader, Michael Harpham, it explores the different ways in which progress can be made in the classroom and how it can be more effectively delivered, identified, evidenced, measured and assessed.

The book provides an overview of progress in schools for both teachers and school leaders, including what is meant by progress and what it looks like in lessons, as well as its implications on assessment, leadership, and internal and external school evaluation. It offers over thirty situation-driven strategies and activities to help develop and deliver progress in and beyond the classroom, focussing on five measures:

- Skills

- Knowledge

- Accuracy

- Resilience

- Independent learning

Full of tips to help improve progress in schools, this is essential reading for all teachers, school leaders and parents.

Michael Harpham is the Director of School Leader Development Ltd and a former Headteacher.

Progress Plain and Simple

What Every Teacher Needs To Know About Improving Pupil Progress

Michael Harpham

Routledge
Taylor & Francis Group

LONDON AND NEW YORK

First published 2020
by Routledge
2 Park Square, Milton Park, Abingdon, Oxon OX14 4RN

and by Routledge
52 Vanderbilt Avenue, New York, NY 10017

Routledge is an imprint of the Taylor & Francis Group, an informa business

©2020 Michael Harpham

The right of Michael Harpham to be identified as author of this work has been asserted by him in accordance with sections 77 and 78 of the Copyright, Designs and Patents Act 1988.

All rights reserved. No part of this book may be reprinted or reproduced or utilised in any form or by any electronic, mechanical, or other means, now known or hereafter invented, including photocopying and recording, or in any information storage or retrieval system, without permission in writing from the publishers.

Trademark notice: Product or corporate names may be trademarks or registered trademarks, and are used only for identification and explanation without intent to infringe.

British Library Cataloguing-in-Publication Data
A catalogue record for this book is available from the British Library

Library of Congress Cataloging-in-Publication Data
Names: Harpham, Michael, author.
Title: Progress plain and simple: what every teacher needs to know about improving pupil progress / Michael Harpham.
Description: Abingdon, Oxon; New York: Routledge, 2020. |
Includes bibliographical references and index.
Identifiers: LCCN 2019049952 (print) | LCCN 2019049953 (ebook) |
ISBN 9780367339647 (hardback) | ISBN 9780367339661 (paperback) |
ISBN 9780429323096 (ebook)
Subjects: LCSH: Teacher effectiveness. | Learning, Psychology of. |
School improvement programs. | Effective teaching.
Classification: LCC LB1025.3 .H3785 2020 (print) | LCC LB1025.3 (ebook) |
DDC 371.102—dc23
LC record available at https://lccn.loc.gov/2019049952
LC ebook record available at https://lccn.loc.gov/2019049953

ISBN: 978-0-367-33964-7 (hbk)
ISBN: 978-0-367-33966-1 (pbk)
ISBN: 978-0-429-32309-6 (ebk)

Typeset in Melior
by codeMantra

Dedicated to all the pupils and teachers with whom I have had the pleasure and privilege to work.

And to the memory of Jane Havell.

Contents

Acknowledgements

This book draws on my experience of education over twenty-five years, as a teacher, school leader, headteacher and consultant in London and the south-east of England. From the many talented students, teachers and leaders I have met along the way, I have learnt so much. They are too many to mention individually here, but their actions and their words are all represented and encapsulated in this book.

As it is often said, life is a journey, not a destination; enriched and occasionally influenced by our fellow travellers. The genesis of this book is no exception. Specific thanks must go to …

Ludovico Tejan, Tracey-Ann Bond and the staff at the Deanes School, without whom this book would never have seen the light of day.

Michael Phillips and Jack Ryan-Phillips for pointing me in the right direction and helping me get a spark of an idea out into the world.

Susan Service, Omar Wallen, Tom Hogarth, Liam Errington, Alan King, Ignacio Castillo, Richard Robinson, Mina Taqvi, Ben Drake, Anban Naidoo, Julia Stubbs and the staff at Arts and Media School, Islington and Juliette Jackson, Moya Richardson and the team at Our Lady's Catholic Primary School in Camden for their invaluable insights and input.

Jon Tait, Paul Ramsey, Jane Hart, Joe Omar, Bukky Yusuf and Claire Waites for their expert wisdom and encouraging guidance during the process.

Caroline Davies for the perfectly captured illustrations.

Dame Sally Coates and Sir John Dunford for their kind permission to quote them.

Annamarie Kino-Wylam and Ann Klein at Routledge for their expertise in guiding me through the whole process.

Finally, to Dad, Christine and Julian, for their enduring love, patience and steadfast support.

Heartfelt thanks to all.

About the author

With twenty-five years teaching experience, fifteen of those at senior leadership level, including headship, in a broad range of schools in London and the Home Counties, Michael has extensive educational and leadership experience to share. In addition, with two master's degrees and completing a doctorate in education, he also brings significant authority and ability to his work.

His passion is for education. As well as working in schools during the day, he has been a school governor and set up his own consultancy, School Leader Development Ltd, to develop and deliver training programmes for teachers and school leaders. He also enjoys supporting and developing staff and teams to reach their potential and, as such, is a highly experienced mentor and coach.

Michael grew up in Yorkshire and went on to study singing, piano and composition at the Royal Academy of Music in London. When not working, he continues to enjoy the artistic side of life, especially photography (published by the *Sunday Times*) and music (performing his own work at the Royal Albert Hall).

Other hobbies include hiking up mountains (he successfully climbed Kilimanjaro for a school charity) and travelling (blogged across India and spent a year on a Fulbright Exchange with the British Council teaching Music in California).

Progress Plain and Simple is his first book.

Progress: just before you enter the classroom – a little background

Progress: introduction

Introduction

When you were a pupil, who were the teachers you remember as making a positive difference to you and your learning? What did they do that was different, special and memorable? Was it a specific lesson, a key moment when the penny dropped, or a life-changing piece of advice? Either way, I am guessing that you will be thinking of those teachers now and hazard an even bigger guess that you remember their names, who they are and what they said and did.

This is the impact that those moments of great teaching have on all of us; moments that are life-changing, inspirational and memorable. This is the goal of this book. To help create more opportunities in lessons where every teacher and every pupil in every school experience magical moments of learning that will stay with them for the rest of their lives.

There is a vast amount of research available about progress, attainment and achievement in schools. Much of it is complex, theoretical, academic or written with a data-proficient professional in mind, all of which is valid. However, the people who really matter and can make the most difference in helping a pupil achieve their potential are the teachers, the parents, the school leaders and not least, the pupils themselves. Thus, in writing this book, it was important for me to write in a way that everyone can access and understand. This book therefore offers a plain and simple look at how learning progresses in the classroom and, as a result, helps everyone involved in helping pupils learn have clearer, more effective conversations about the progress.

Why this book is needed

Even after millennia of research into education, we appear to be no nearer finding the holy grail of education. We still do not appear to have the magic formula that teachers can use in lessons and ensure that all their pupils learn everything they're taught and pass every exam they take with flying colours.

With progress being *the* measure of success for school effectiveness (Reynolds et al., 2014), until such a formula is found, teachers and schools must look to themselves and others for ideas and answers. This book offers a fresh, current perspective on a universal, age-old theme, by looking at progress in education today; what it looks like, what the current educational themes and variations are in relation to progress and what they mean for pupils, teachers, school leaders and parents.

Whilst there is much written about progress in various shapes and forms, there doesn't appear to be a book that brings the diverse thoughts, writings and musings on progress together.

This book attempts to bring the most current thoughts and writings around progress in schools together and offer some further clarity on it.

Further, just like it is important for any established company to regularly review and update its policies, so that they know what they are doing is best practice and fit-for-purpose, I think it is important to do the same by writing this book, reviewing and updating our educational practice around the most important measure of success for any educational establishment – the progress of its pupils.

Last, but not least, in 2016, teachers in the UK were working on average 52.6 hours a week, compared to 45.9 hours a week in 2013, an increase of 15% (Higton, 2016). In addition, 93% of respondents said that workload was at least a fairly serious problem, with over half (52%) saying it was a very serious problem. I have no reason to believe this issue has gone away since then. If this book helps (in)experienced teachers and school leaders save a few hours of additional work by being a go-to book for ideas, advice and guidance that they know will work, then my work here is more than justified.

Our experience of progress in school

When interviewing potential teachers and leaders, I have a favourite question to ask: "I tend to walk around school and look in on lessons to see what learning is taking place. If I walked into one of your lessons, how would I see progress being made?"

A reasonable question I hear you think.

Indeed, I think so too. However, rarely do I hear an answer that is as complete, as accurate or as clear as it could be.

When I was at school in the 1970s, teachers taught, and pupils learnt. If the pupils did well, that was great. If they didn't, they didn't. Such was the education system then, and how it had been for decades before.

In the late 1970s and 1980s with the arrival of Margaret Thatcher and her conservative government, a new order was brought into education. Within two decades and an unprecedented centralisation of power and control, the government increased their grip on education with far more measurement and accountability of schools.

Since then, and with little changed by subsequent governments, the currency of accountability and target-setting in education is progress, especially, the quantitative currency of numbers, levels, test scores and grades.

The work of the teacher, school leader and headteacher today only has currency and validity if the language has a smattering of numbers; preferably upwardly mobile numbers.

The purpose of this book, in response to Biesta's excellent and still relevant challenge to schools today (Biesta, 2008), is to re-find our enjoyment, awe and wonder in teaching and learning; provide a "good" education for all our young people that stacks up as "effective"; and remind ourselves that education is literally a *wonder-ful* journey to be experienced, not just a profit-and-loss balance sheet to be justified.

In schools today, we are clear about three things: teaching is still the largest influence on a pupil making progress (Coates, 2015, p.84), the most important influence on a pupil's progress is the quality of the teacher (Lenon, 2017, p.55), and there is a marked difference between poor and great teaching (Slater, Davies and Burgess, 2009).

Thus, the focus of this book: progress plain and simple.

I wish I'd had this book as a new teacher to give me easy-to-use ideas and strategies that worked. I wish I'd had a book like this as a new head of department and senior leader to help me get the best from my team. I wish my parents had had a book like this to help them support me, my brother and sister with our education.

This book then is for teachers. It offers an alternative perspective on teaching, learning and progress. I hope, as a result of this book, both experienced and inexperienced teachers can more easily recognise and celebrate those wonderful, fabulous moments in their lessons when we see pupils "getting it", when the penny drops, when the lightbulb comes on and when we explicitly see progress being made.

This is a book for school leaders. Almost every school leader today operates in a world where data is king. However, data comes from assessments: tests of teaching and learning. More testing creating more numbers will not necessarily create more learning and see more progress being made. Only improvements in teaching and learning will do this.

This book seeks to help school leaders more effectively identify and address issues in the progress of teaching and learning. In reading this book, I hope, as a result, that the learning walks, book scrutinies and general monitoring of school life more effectively enable school leaders to see at a glance the progress being made in their school.

This book is also for parents because much of what they hear from schools, the government or the media about progress can be almost impossible to connect with their own experience of school or their own daily experience of their child (Hattie, 2009). I hope in reading this book, parents come to know and understand a little more of what teachers are talking about, in real language, in real life, and in the real world.

Features of the book and how it can be used

The first section of the book gives an overview of progress in schools, including what we mean by progress and progress over time in education. The second section is aimed at schoolteachers and leaders, offering over 30 strategies and activities to help develop and deliver progress in the classroom. These strategies and activities are situation driven. The teacher or leader should use them when the situation requires. They are not a panacea, nor are they a set of requirements to be implemented en masse. The third section is aimed at teachers, school leaders and governors, offering fresh perspectives on progress across the school, on assessment, on leadership and on internal and external school evaluation in relation to progress.

This book then helps clarify what progress in schools is, what progress looks like in lessons in lessons over time, and how that progress could be more effectively demonstrated and assessed. The aim is to enable teachers, pupils, school leaders and parents have more meaningful conversations about progress and therefore add to the larger educational discussion around progress.

Summary

In summary, the aim of the book is to help schools, heads of department, and teachers understand what progress and progress over time is and what that means for teaching and learning. It unpacks what challenge and progress look like in lessons for teachers learners, and the learning process. Its aim is to help teachers understand what they can (continue to) do individually and collectively to ensure all their pupils are sufficiently challenged and find meaningful activities that are clear, explicit and measurable.

This book is not an exact science.

This book is not a specific, nor the only way of being.

In a style borrowed from a well-known film, I hope you enjoy the book.

I hope that future lessons in classrooms around the world are better and clearer as a result.

I hope greater progress is made by our young people as a result of this little book.

From small acorns, great oaks grow.

I hope.

2 Progress: defined

Progress plain and simple:

Progress in learning is the level of change a pupil manages to achieve in the amount of knowledge and/or skills they can demonstrate in a lesson.

In this chapter we will cover:

- Definitions of progress
- The importance of challenge and pace in lessons
- Transmission v transference

Introduction

So, if you walked into a lesson, how would you see progress being made?

Would it be in the lit-up faces of the pupils in a science class, predicting how an experiment was going to unfold and seeing the wonder in watching the experiment go as they predicted?

Would it be in the forest of hands, reaching for the stars as the pupils want to answer the question the teacher has just posed, keen to show their new understanding?

Would it be in the earnest scratching of pen on paper as 30 pupils are engrossed in their next few paragraphs of creative writing?

Or would it be in the quiet patience of a pupil walking over to help teach another pupil how to play the next few bars of a piece of music on the piano?

This is how we see progress being made in a lesson.

Definitions of progress

It is important at the outset that we have a clear definition of what we mean by progress. If something is to be plain and simple, it needs to be crystal clear. Hence, the following to help us both be clear about what we are discussing in this book.

Progress is defined by the Oxford English Dictionary (OED) as: "Forward or onward movement towards a destination; a development towards an improved or more advanced condition; move forward or onward in space or time". Its Latin roots literally mean "walk forward". Thus, we are concerned with the work of pupils in school that takes them forward or onward.

Secondly, progress in what? Specifically, learning. This, the OED defines as "the acquisition of knowledge or skills through study, experience, or being taught". Thus, on the one hand we acquire, have an increase in the *amount* of knowledge and skills we learn. On the other hand, learning is also about the process of acquisition, *how* we gain that knowledge and those skills. That's the focus of this book. How we learn.

But how do we know the amount of learning or skill is sufficient? How do we know we have achieved? This brings us to our third definition: achievement. This is defined as "a thing done successfully with effort, skill, or courage; to successfully bring about or reach (a desired objective or result) by effort, skill, or courage". With its French roots meaning to bring to a head.

Thus, we have an increase in skills or knowledge that is acquired sufficiently. This suggests that there must be a measure of success. And that measure of success must be clear, not only to the teacher but also to the learner.

Another word often found alongside achievement is pupil attainment. It is worth pausing here and being clear what we mean by this. The OED defines attainment as "success in achieving (something that one has worked for), to reach (a specified age, size, or amount)". This suggests a learner getting there, reaching a destination successfully against a particular measure.

This is frequently and most often demonstrated in schools through assessment. To assess is defined as "to evaluate or estimate the nature, ability, or quality of; calculate or estimate the price or value of". With its Latin root meaning "to sit by".

So, to state our definition of progress clearly and simply, we are interested in the forward movement of a pupil's learning in the acquisition of skills and knowledge, through effort, skill and courage, to successfully reach a desired destination.

Progress as challenge and transference over time

Teachers around the world, day in, day out, stand in front of their pupils and say "Morning all. Please turn to page 35 in your textbooks", or in more technologically advanced schools, "Morning all. Please complete the starter activity on the white board". However a lesson starts, there is always the potential for it to be no more than copying from the book or the (not-so-interactive) whiteboard.

But teaching and learning are more than just copying from PowerPoint presentations and textbooks. These are receptacles of knowledge and help teachers clarify,

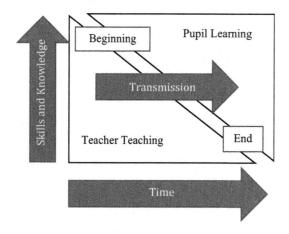

Figure 2.1 Transmission During a Lesson

and pupils understand, the topics being taught. However, the learning from this experience is in what pupils do with the information or skills; how they can make the implicit learning demonstrably explicit. It is in the teacher bringing the learning to life for the pupils, so that they can fully understand, see and engage with the learning for themselves. There are two conceptual frameworks which help illustrate this point.

First, we have transmission during a lesson.

Figure 2.1 illustrates the teacher teaching (symbolised by the triangle to the left) to the pupils (symbolised by the triangle to the right) through copying a PowerPoint presentation or reading and writing from the worksheets or the textbook. Thus, the teacher transmits the information to the pupils. But this is the transmission of information and with minimal checking on the part of the teacher, not necessarily the transference of learning they would expect. Without checking, there is a risk of a disconnect between the teaching and the learning.

Just like a radio mast transmits radio signals to be received by a radio receiver, whilst there might be challenge within the learning, and takes time to read and understand it, there is minimal engagement with or transference to the pupil of that learning. How is the teacher *checking* that learning has taken place? How are pupils *demonstrating* their learning? This can be a common problem for inexperienced teachers who might perceive teaching to be preparing and delivering PowerPoint presentations, rarely taking the chance to check and enable pupils to demonstrate their learning.

Figure 2.2 more accurately illustrates what progress is. It is about the transference of learning. This comes about mainly from the teacher. A PowerPoint presentation or textbook may be involved, but these are instruments to the learning and are a small part of the actual lesson itself.

Teachers need to move from transmitting learning through PowerPoints and books, and deliver a lesson or a scheme of work over time, which is increasingly challenging and increasingly difficult, with the teacher consciously transferring the knowledge, skills and learning to the pupil.

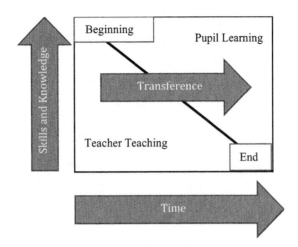

Figure 2.2 Transference During a Lesson

This is the point of this book, that effective learning is delivered through the deliberate, considered transference of learning through a lesson, where knowledge and skills are transferred over time through the teacher to the learner. In John Hattie's words "visible learning" (Hattie, 2012). The difference between this book and John Hattie's work is that I am not just concerned with visible learning *but a consciously driven, visible learning process.*

Sufficient challenge in the classroom

Challenge in the classroom is the upward movement of learning; the harder, more difficult, more complex work that we learn over time. The OED defines challenge as "the new or difficult task that tests somebody's ability and skill".

A useful metaphor may be the vertical-ness of a step as you gain height when climbing a mountain. The steeper the climb, the swifter the gain in height, the harder the challenge facing you. Thus, the difficulty, complexity and hardness of an activity build in the challenge to a lesson and helps pupils make progress. To prepare pupils for the difficulty and complexity of skills and knowledge that they will be facing in a lesson, it is possible to do this in two ways.

First, it is possible to prepare them for the challenges facing them by explaining that they relate to previously learnt skills and knowledge. Just like climbing a mountain, when a young climber may have previously successfully climbed smaller hills or completed shorter walks and therefore had overcome similar challenges in the past, so we refer to those experiences to help the pupil focus and connect with the challenges that lie ahead. They may be more challenging and more complex than previous challenges, but they are not new (Figure 2.3).

A possibly unique perspective to illustrate this is in relating the transference process to the Hegelian Dialectic. Pupils of philosophy will have come across Hegel, the 19th-century philosopher. In his theory, he presents a thesis of how we learn or know more. To develop our understanding (our thesis), there needs to be

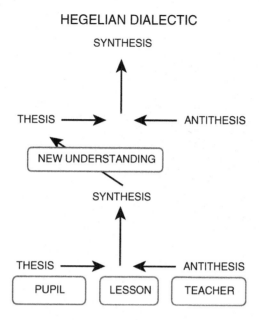

HEGELIAN DIALECTIC

Figure 2.3 The Hegelian Dialectic

challenge to that understanding (an antithesis). In challenging this thesis with an antithesis, with something opposite, comes about a bringing together of both, and a new way of understanding things (synthesis). This new understanding, knowledge or skill becomes the new thesis, to be challenged at a higher level with a new antithesis, which again is synthesised to produce a new synthesis of understanding, skill and knowledge.

This is the fundamental of iterative learning; building on previously learnt work with successively more complex, more difficult challenges and help pupils master increasingly more difficult, more challenging work.

If we take this theory into the classroom, for example, into a Music class, the teacher may present a lesson on the Blues. To learn about the Blues, it would be helpful to draw on previous knowledge. For example, pupils having previously learnt about improvising on a scale when studying Chinese music or jazz would find improvising in a Blues piece around a six-note scale (the Blues scale), relatively less challenging than at first thought.

Making use of Hegel's Dialectic helps pupils understand that future learning is built on and based around previous learning and therefore new learning is just a continuation of previous learning and, as a result, need be nowhere near as scary or frightening. As a result, pupils are more likely to engage far more readily and therefore make far faster progress than would otherwise be the case (Figure 2.4).

Another possibly unique perspective to illustrate the process of facing challenges and learning new knowledge is in relating this process to Vygotsky's Zone of Proximal Development.

This framework enables learners to jump in at the deep end into new learning and helps pupils to swim with increasing intellectual confidence and skill. The Zone of

Independence: Can do
independently

Acceptance: Can do if
guided

Resistance: Can't do,
even if guided

Figure 2.4 Vygotsky's Zone of Proximal Development

Proximal Development helps pupils to understand skills and knowledge that were previously unknown.

The first stage is where a pupil can't do anything, even if guided. There is a lack of understanding of the basic principles that underpin a new skill or new knowledge. With further teacher support, the pupil comes to a better understanding of the skills, knowledge, concepts and the intellectual framework that supports the learning. Therefore, the pupil moves from a "can't do" to a "can-do" position but still needs to be guided.

According to Vygotsky, this is where the most learning takes place.

The final step in the learning process is the conscious withdrawal of teacher support, enabling the full independence of the learner to occur. As confidence grows, so the pupil takes their first independent steps with this new learning and as a result show progress.

Thus, Vygotsky's Zone of Proximal Development helps illustrate the process of learning something new; pupils moving from a place of fear, where they have no idea of what is happening, no understanding of what to do, to being able to work independently and confidently.

If challenge provides the difficulty of the work in hand, the curriculum map (framework of learning over a key stage), programme of study (schedule of learning over a year) and scheme of work (schedule of learning over a topic) offer a structured time frame that determines the pace of the work in hand. These will be covered in more detail in Chapter 4.

> Through the activities devised for the lesson, the teacher provides *challenge* through the increasing difficulty of the activities set and *pace* through a planned and constructed curriculum in the scheme of work, programme of study and curriculum map.

Chapters 5–9 present several strategies and activities that help demonstrate explicit learning, explicit transference and therefore explicit progress.

3 The theory of progress

Progress plain and simple:

Progress in learning is a forward or onward movement towards a curriculum destination. It is the educational development towards an improved or more advanced condition.

In this chapter, we will cover what the research says about:

- Progress in relation to teaching and learning
- Progress in relation to the curriculum
- Progress in relation to assessment
- Progress in relation to accountability

Introduction

In this chapter, we look at what key writers and researchers have to say about progress. Whilst not being an exhaustive overview, it will give the reader a good idea of the key themes related to progress that emerge.

> Progress is the forward movement of learning: the understanding of more knowledge, the acquisition of more skills, the catching up, the filling the gaps and the overcoming of more barriers. All are concerned with learning *more* (Third Space Learning, 2019). Why do we need to learn more? Because the evidence suggests that progress at school makes a difference to future job prospects and future income (Hunt and Vernoit, 2014), and it is *the* criterion when measuring school effectiveness (Reynolds et al., 2014).

Progress in schools can be viewed in different ways. It may be experienced as an integrated teaching and learning process (Dunford, 2016, p.69), a curriculum that is structured, coherent and regularly reviewed (Ofsted, 2019b), knowing each pupil and how they work best (Dann, 2016), or the development of micro skills that secure incremental improvements in learning (Stigler and Hiebert, 1999, Paas, 2003).

> With there being no one, prescribed method of teaching (Tomsett, 2015, Wilshaw, 2016) and multiple definitions of learning, which are wide-ranging and complex (Illeris, 2007, p.20), it is clear why our definition and understanding of progress is unclear (Ofsted, 2017).

Thus, with such disparity of meaning, there is a need for a unifying, shared language amongst teachers, pupils, school leaders and parents around progress, so that research and conversations can be more meaningful as a result (Stigler and Hiebert, 1999, Fielding and Moss, 2011, Swann et al., 2012).

A clear theme related to progress in the research is that schools need to set and achieve targets and define their (and their pupils') progress by the measurement of outcomes (DfEE, 2001, Kelly, 2011, Coates, 2015), or what is now known as "performativity". As a result, progress in schools is a major issue both educationally and politically.

This leads to a question of balance. How much time and effort should teachers and school leaders expend on paying to Caesar what belongs to Caesar, acquiescing to the pressure from government, parents and school inspectors to "perform", measuring progress through quantitative assessments? Or by fulfilling our obligation to pupils to give them the best education in our power; to provide a high-quality education for all that delivers enriching, empowering teaching and measuring progress through qualitative assessments (Silva, 2008, Fielding and Moss, 2011, Solomon, 2015)?

Some would argue that the balance has now tipped too far in the wrong direction (Ofsted, 2017).

Progress in relation to teaching

Teaching matters. Teaching is the most important factor in securing pupil progress.

According to several researchers, teaching in the classroom is the single most important factor in school effectiveness with pupil progress being the yardstick by which teacher quality is assessed (Stigler and Hiebert, 1999, Hattie, 2012, Sutton Trust, 2015, Tomsett, 2015, Hood, 2017, Ofsted, 2019a). However, interestingly, there is little research into effective primary or secondary school teaching in the UK (Galton, 1980).

Kyriakides and Creemers (2008) identified that it is not the length of time a teacher remains at a school that secures good teaching, but the consistency of their effectiveness, with teachers who do particularly well with one class, more likely to do so with other classes. Similarly, Kane et al. (2010) in their research found that a teacher's past track record of results was the best way of ascertaining a teacher's effectiveness, no matter which key stage or subject they taught. And pupils know who the good teachers are. Who doesn't remember their best (and worst!) teachers?

Dylan Wiliam concluded that demographic factors account for most between school variation in teaching and learning and that schools don't make a difference (Kyriakides and Creemers, 2008, Wiliam, 2011, Lenon, 2016). However, there is the largest variation between classrooms within a school (Muijs, 2014, Hattie, 2015); therefore, the biggest variation is between teachers. He found that in the UK, variability at the classroom level is at least *four times* that at school level. Therefore, if you go to school, it doesn't matter very much which school you go to, but it matters very much which classrooms you are in (Reynolds et al., 2014).

This concurred with an earlier piece of research by Hanushek and Rivkin (2006), who found that pupils taught by the most effective teacher in a group of 50 teachers learn in six months what those taught by the average teacher in a group learn in a year. However, pupils taught by the least effective teacher in that group of 50 teachers will take two years to achieve the same learning (Muijs, 2003, Hamre & Pianta, 2005).

Therefore, the effectiveness of a teacher is a strong predictor of pupil progress throughout school, and having a succession of strong or weak teachers can have lasting effects (Creemers, 1994, Muijs and Reynolds, 2003, Kyriakides and Creemers, 2008, Muijs et al., 2014, Reynolds et al., 2014).

Thus, helping create higher quality teachers helps pupils make more progress (Stigler and Hiebert, 1999). Higher quality teachers are especially important with lower ability pupils (Muijs, 2003, Aaronson, 2007, Jahan, 2010).

As a result, to improve progress, we need to improve the variation in teaching. In other words, an effective school is a school full of effective classrooms. Thus, for school leaders to have an impact on progress, they need to reduce the variability between classrooms and improve the consistency of teaching (Hattie, 2015).

Wiliam is cynical about the possibility of this, finding that left on their own, teachers improve slowly (5% over 20 years), recommending the need for increased teacher Continuing Professional Development on progress (Wiliam, 2011, Hood, 2017).

> However, later research has found that formative assessment and coaching were particularly effective in helping teachers improve in the classroom (Muijs et al., 2014, Hattie, 2015, Dudek et al., 2019).

In my experience, I concur with this. It is a rare school that does not have some teacher and leader expertise on which to draw within it. So, rather than sending staff out on expensive external training courses, schools should buddy them up with a strong teacher or leader to coach them until they are as good.

Further, with middle leadership often called the "engine room" of a school, what better place to start to improve progress in teaching and learning in a school? Schools need to make sure that there are frequent (every fortnight) meetings between senior and middle leaders, enabling them to share best practice and ensure consistency of leadership, teaching and learning across the school (Hattie, 2015).

What makes great teaching

Teaching can be difficult to define, and teaching taking place does not necessarily mean learning is taking place (Tomsett, 2015, Wilshaw, 2016). Researchers are clear that there is no prescribed method of teaching. What follows is a resume of what researchers and professionals surmise as to what makes high-quality teaching.

The Teachers' Standards (DfE, 2011) are a set of standards which the government laid out in 2011 as the benchmark for the minimum standard expected in the profession. All trainee and practising teachers are expected to evidence and meet these standards to enter and continue to work in the profession.

The standards are very good at clarifying *what* is expected of teachers in the classroom (e.g. develop pupils' skills and knowledge), but there is less clarity as to *how* teachers can do this.

In summary, the standards are as follows:

- Set high expectations which inspire, motivate and challenge pupils

- Promote good progress and outcomes by pupils

- Demonstrate good subject and curriculum knowledge

- Plan and teach well-structured lessons

- Adapt teaching to respond to the strengths and needs of all pupils

- Make accurate and productive use of assessment

- Manage behaviour effectively to ensure a good and safe learning environment

- Fulfil wider professional responsibilities

Researchers concur that setting high expectations, giving high-quality instruction and remaining constantly challenging is universally the key to securing great teaching and supporting the pupils who need it (Coe, 2014, Coates, 2015, Hattie, 2015, Tomsett, 2015, Lenon, 2016).

With a didactical difference in a class being up to four years (Deunk et al., 2015), *in-class differentiation has little impact* on significantly improving pupil attainment (Scheerens and Bosker, 1997, Hattie, 2009). In a move from what some teachers may regard as sacrosanct, the research suggests that high-quality teaching does *not* set lower expectations to different pupils (i.e. all must, most should, some could...), does *not* set different tasks for different groups of pupils (this adds to teacher work load) and does *not* set different tasks for different learning styles (Curry, 1990, Gardner, 1993, Pashler, 2008, Willingham, 2010, Ofsted, 2019a). On the latter point, as Reiner and Willingham succinctly put it "Pupils may have preferences about how to learn, but no evidence suggests that catering to those preferences will lead to better learning" (Riener and Willingham, 2010). However, adapting teaching techniques and classroom activities in a responsive way does (Curry, 1990, Deunk et al., 2015, Education Endowment Foundation, 2019c).

In addition, teachers need to be passionate about their subject. With a strong relationship between subject knowledge and attainment, teachers need to have good subject, pedagogical and pedagogical subject knowledge (Cordingley, 2015, Ofsted, 2019a). It almost goes without saying, but the clarity of lesson presentation is also consistently related to pupils' attainment (Rosenshine, 1986, Muijs and Reynolds, 2017). Effective teachers can communicate clearly and directly with their pupils, without going beyond pupils' levels of comprehension (Smith and Land, 1981, Walberg, 1986, Muijs and Reynolds, 2003, Muijs et al., 2010).

In this way, the teacher's ability to promote questioning and feedback, checking on pupils' learning rather than giving extended lectures (Kyriakides and Creemers, 2008) is key to develop learning and the pupils' mastery of the subject with strong empirical evidence to support this (Rosenshine, 1986, Brophy and Good, 1986, Creemers, 1994, Askew and William, 1995, Smith et al., 2004, Coe, 2014, Muijs and Reynolds, 2017, Ofsted, 2019a).

Finally, whilst the teachers' standards are rightly a set of standards by which professionals are judged, they are very much located with the teacher and teaching. I would argue that the definition of a great teacher is in their ability to produce great learning. Therefore, there is a need for the Teachers' Standards to more explicitly emphasise the other half of the equation, namely the great learning that needs to occur as a result of the great teaching.

Progress: the transference process between teacher and pupil

> So, it is by returning to the essence of the task – that transfer of knowledge and skill from one to another – that we spot both the simplicity and the complexity of the task of teaching.
>
> (Coates, 2015, p.84)

Transference is the conscious intellectual movement or interactive process by the teacher, in taking pupils from one place to another, both aware of the process involved. Like a coach, the teacher designs a series of activities that will move the pupil from their current state to the goal state (Galton, 1980, Swann, 1988, Wiliam, 2011, Hattie, 2012, Coates, 2015). As John Dewey so succinctly puts it in his pedagogic creed (1897), "I believe that education is a *process* of living and not a *preparation* for future living". Hence, *teachers* manage the learning process; *learners* respond to it.

As can be seen in Figure 3.1, the learning process of the pupil in the classroom starts with an interactive, external engagement with the teacher or the outside world. Then through the learning process of questioning and giving and receiving feedback, the pupil is able to digest and internalise the learning.

> The teacher in the classroom instigates the learning taking place with the best strategy.
> The teacher manages both the teaching and the learning process.
> Learning cannot take place without the active engagement of every pupil with that strategy.
> Increased engagement = increased opportunities to learn (Kirschner, 2006, Illeris, 2007, Hattie, 2015).

Further, regarding the transference of knowledge, which is external, fixed and constructed/co-constructed by the pupil and teacher (Hargreaves, 2010, p.224), there is a need for the teacher to check and ensure that not only has their teaching been transmitted but has also transferred; that the pupil has taken on board the information that needs to be learnt and understood. As Sweller et al. (2011) point out about the effectiveness of the process, "if nothing in the long-term memory has been altered, nothing has been learned". This chimes with Swann et al.'s findings

Figure 3.1 The Learning Process

in their transformability model (Swann, 2012, p.6) with teachers and pupils actively working together in an environment of trust and collaboration to ultimately secure deep learning.

The importance of getting lessons right reminds me of the saying "Take care of the pennies, and the pounds will take care of themselves". John Hattie (2009) identifies making teaching and learning as visible as possible as a way of securing more successful lessons. For the process to be as effective as possible in lessons, being clear, explicit and as "visible" as possible helps, but it is also in the teacher consciously, *actively* driving the process of learning forward that adds to further progress being secured. It is not just about visible teaching and learning through the lesson but about visible progress through the process.

However, effective transference has been hampered by pressure from a government insistent on teachers monitoring pupil progress as opposed to helping pupils become owners of their own learning (Kelly, 2011, Christodoulou, 2016). Regardless of that external pressure on the process, it is to the interface of teacher and learner that we turn next: the lesson.

Progress in relation to lessons

> Lessons are the heartbeat of a school. The success or failure of a school will ultimately depend on the activity within the classroom.
>
> (Coates, 2015, p.86)

Learning objectives or learning outcomes?

An interesting view on learning objectives (the focus of a lesson) is that some writers prefer to see them focused, clear and challenging, whilst others prefer a descriptor as to what is to be learnt (Lindvall and Nitko, 1975, Coates, 2015, Tomsett 2015). In any lesson, consistency is key; applying clear, shared routines with pupils will win the day (Coates, 2015).

Therefore, it is important to keep learning objectives focused and clear, to keep the end point and purpose always in mind (Stigler and Hiebert, 1999, Biesta, 2008, Ofsted, 2019a). To this end, a plenary, the counterpart to the learning objective, is an excellent way to sum up a lesson and confirm how effectively the aim of the lesson was achieved (Swann, 1988, Tomsett, 2015).

The importance of group work

There is strong empirical evidence that group work is integral to effective instruction in a lesson (Creemers, 1994, Cohen 2014). In their meta-analysis of group work in mathematics, Capar and Tarim (2015) concluded that group work was categorically more effective in learning maths than a traditional method of learning.

> Most writers and researchers agree that group work in a lesson needs to be clearly structured, sequenced and have enough prior knowledge for the participants to engage and discuss their work meaningfully (Cohen and Lotan, 2014, Kutnick and Blatchford, 2014, Capar and Tarim, 2015, Education Endowment Foundation, 2018, Kirschner et al., 2018, Ofsted, 2019a).

Kutnick and Blatchford (2014) recommend that teachers need to have a social understanding of the groups in their classes to ensure effective group work takes place. Providing empirical evidence that their SPRinG approach (Social Pedagogic Research into Groupwork) works, they recommend it as a strategy for improving progress in primary classrooms.

Further, Kirschner (2018) applying his collaborative cognitive load theory (how we work as a group) concludes that teachers, when deciding on whether to use group work as an activity or not, should explicitly state where the pupils are in their learning as a group (novice or expert), how well they work as a group and the effects of the task set (high or low complexity) to achieve the learning objective. It may be that the teacher decides that working as a group is *not* the most effective way of working to achieve those objectives. For further, excellent work in this area, read Cohen and Lotan's (2014) "Designing Groupwork" or Kutnick and Blatchford's (2014) "Effective Group Work in Primary School Classrooms".

Homework

> The educational process's end goal is for pupils to be able to learn, understand and apply that learning on their own. To this end, the empirical research is clear that homework is a strong component of effective instruction (Creemers, 1994, p.94) and can make up to five months improvement in a pupil's progress (EEF 2019b).

However, there are a couple of interesting points to note:

1 British pupils get more homework than their counterparts in many other countries in Europe.

2 Schools in the UK, however, don't have to set homework. There is no statutory requirement for schools to set homework.

3 School inspectors don't inspect homework. Ofsted appear to be uninterested in inspecting homework or researching it in respect of their inspections in schools, with no reference to it in their inspection framework nor their research (Ofsted, 2019b).

When contacted about this, Ofsted replied:

> "Ofsted does not inspect homework in schools. There is no statutory requirement for schools to set homework for pupils, but they may do so as part of school policy. The school inspection handbook does not mention inspections of homework specifically, or the schools' arrangements for setting it."

So, there it is. Schools don't need to set homework and Ofsted won't come looking for it in their inspections.

Looking to the future: technology

We are living in extraordinary times. We are witness to what will be known in history as the third technological revolution. I am old enough (as may be some readers) to remember being taught, and teaching, with chalk and a blackboard, before a world of computers, Microsoft Word, Excel, Google, the internet and mobile phones took over how we communicate and work.

With the teacher in the classroom in control of teaching (and therefore learning), still largely inexperienced with current technology, their pupils are embracing the new technologies and finding a world of information (and therefore knowledge) not available to them in schools. As Halverson (2009) puts it, "The learner revolution takes place (for young people) outside the classroom".

However, schools are increasingly engaging with information technology, making a positive difference to the way they work. Examples include pupils using PowerPoint and Spark video to encapsulate what they have learnt (Lane, 2019); teachers and school leaders using Google documents to co-edit and collaborate contemporaneously with what they are doing, or parents, pupils and teachers accessing key documents remotely and instantaneously through online learning platforms or their school's app: all innovations in education.

Further, Knight (2015) looks forward to working in a world where global access to electronic textbooks means an education open to all. As the average age of teachers reduces, as technology continues its revolution at break-neck speed and as education gradually assimilates these new technologies, I predict that by 2030, the technological revolution will have significantly made its mark on education, bringing both new problems as well as incredible opportunities.

Progress in relation to learning

Having the opportunity to learn correlates particularly positively with attainment (Stallings, 1985, Scheerens and Bosker, 1997, Muijs and Reynolds, 2003, Ofsted 2019a).

Illeris (2007) summarises the four ways in which research regard how we learn. They are through:

- Cumulation (new facts not connected to previous experience and knowledge)

- Assimilation (new facts connected to previous experience and knowledge)

- Accommodation (new facts that require understanding to be reorganised)

- Transformation (new facts that bring a new interpretation or meaning to previous experience and knowledge)

To aid those processes to happen, the teacher chooses a myriad of activities to help that learning to take place. Section 2 of this book explores a number of them that enable progress to be more visible. To help reinforce the learning that takes place, a number of techniques can be used.

> Dunlowsky et al. (2013, p.45) tested ten learning techniques and found that practice testing (self-testing or taking practice tests over to-be-learned material) and distributed practice (implementing a schedule of practice that spreads out study activities over time) scored highly in improving pupils' learning.

Whilst interleaved practice, a schedule of practice that mixes two different but related topics/problems within a single study session (Richland, 2003, Rohrer, 2014), elaborative interrogation (generating an explanation for why an explicitly stated fact or concept is true) and self-explanation (explaining how new information is related to known information, or explaining steps taken during problem solving) were viewed as moderately effective, although according to Dunlowsky, this was due to a lack of extensively available research rather than the techniques themselves being less effective than others.

Finally, summarisation (writing summaries of various lengths of to-be-learned texts), highlighting text (marking potentially important portions of to-be-learned materials while reading), using a keyword mnemonic (using keywords and mental imagery to associate verbal materials), using imagery for text learning (attempting to form mental images of text materials while reading or listening) and re-reading (re-studying text material again after an initial reading) all scored low as to their effectiveness to improve pupils' learning, and therefore should not be overly used in classroom practice (Rawson and Kintsch, 2005).

Progress and the curriculum

> If teaching is the most important factor to effect progress in a school, what teachers teach in the classroom (the curriculum) and outside the classroom (extra-curricular activities) is highly rated also (Silva, 2008).

What teachers are expected to teach (the National Curriculum), including having a strong reading programme (Ofsted, 2017), is not open to debate or discussion. Neither is the structure of the curriculum and the logic and intellectual coherence behind that structure, there being strong empirical evidence that this is a key component in effective instruction (Creemers, 1994, Ofsted, 2017).

There is also an increasing body of empirical evidence that due to the political climate enforcing high-stakes accountability, there has been a narrowing of the curriculum. In recent years, this has been particularly true in Key Stage 2, with teachers teaching to the test, and in secondary schools, of equating the curriculum with the examination board syllabus or statutory test (Jones et al., 2017, Allen, 2018, Ofsted, 2019a).

> In addition, Ofsted recently recognised that there are several deficiencies in the educational system regarding curriculum thinking. "There is limited evidence of a thoughtful approach to the curriculum, which is often equated with the timetable and discussed in a generic fashion. Schools reported that few teachers are trained in curriculum development or theory" (Ofsted, 2019a).

A regular review of the curriculum is therefore recognised as important to pupil progression. In this regard, most schools have a sense of subject-specific progression in their schemes of work. However, between subjects and more holistically across the school, there appears to be less coherence and a lack of a shared language to discuss the curriculum (Stigler and Hiebert, 1999, Ofsted, 2019a).

> Having a scheme of work or programme of study that maps out the curriculum and the necessary assessments over time in a logical way will bring much needed coherence. Having a consistent format to progressive and comprehensive lesson plans and schemes of work, etc. will improve progress experienced in the classroom (Coates, 2015, Dunford, 2016, Christodoulou, 2016). Consistency is key. Further, by having clear end points and a clear focus as to what the product of a scheme of work or programme of study are, will go some way to bringing much needed focus and purpose to education (Biesta, 2008, Ofsted, 2019a).

Researchers recommend increasing the use of textbooks, an authoritative and incrementally progressive scheme of work if ever there was one (Stigler and Hiebert, 1999, Paas, 2003, Knight, 2015), rather than using exam specifications which some heads of department (erroneously) think need little amending as a scheme of work.

Rather surprisingly, only 10% of primary school teachers use textbooks (Christodoulou, 2016), compared to Finland (95%) and Singapore (70%), two of the most successful countries in the world, regularly promoted as exemplar education systems. There is huge potential here for significant improvement in an area that matters.

Progress in relation to assessment

Overall, the purpose of assessment is to improve standards, not merely to measure them.

(Ofsted, 2003)

Why should we assess pupils' work? As the learning process produces changes in the skills, knowledge and behaviour of the learner, frequent assessment helps measure and make explicit how much progress has been made (Lindvall and Nitko, 1975, Hattie, 2009). Further, with intelligence and motivation contributing 83% to the prediction of future achievement (Kriegbaum et al., 2018), assessments are therefore a reliable indicator of possible future achievement.

More specifically, assessment:

■ Creates *clarity* as to what is being taught and learnt

■ Creates more *certainty* as to what is being taught and learnt

■ Creates *pace* in teaching and learning

■ Creates *consistency* of learning between classes and schools

■ Creates a *measure of progress* and therefore a perception of progress

■ Helps create a *plan and structure* to teaching and learning

(Dann, 2016, Muijs and Reynolds, 2017, EEF, 2019a)

Figure 3.2 The Assessment Process

As summarised in Figure 3.2, assessment tests the pupil's ability to remember and recognise information. It can take two main forms – formative assessment (helping inform or form further learning) and summative assessment (summarising what's been learnt). In more detail:

> Progress can be measured through diagnostic assessment, part of the internal formative stage, whereby the teacher determines how well a class seem to have learnt a particular lesson; through formative assessment, by pupils demonstrating how quickly they understand something and through summative assessment by testing internally or externally what has been learnt to date (Galton, 1980). The teacher may give the same test for both a formative and summative test, but it is in the *use* of the data that is produced that makes the test formative or summative (EEF, 2019a).

Diagnostic assessment

Diagnostic assessment helps teachers understand specifically how well pupils have learnt something and helps them to uncover areas of weakness and therefore aid further development (Satterly, 1989).

> It is most useful to inform lesson planning and delivery (Lindvall and Nitko, 1975, Satterly, 1989) whereby the teacher *screens* the class to determine whether learning problems exist; *describes* the nature of the problem; *analyses* the specific difficulty, *hypothesises* as to the solution, *plans* for the solution and *evaluates* how well the pupils have done, sometimes, all in a few minutes. This area of assessment is little used (Quigley, 2016, EEFa, 2019), under-researched (Dann, 2016), a central aspect to effective teaching around the world (Reynolds et al., 2014) and important (MacCallum, 2000, Muijs et al., 2014, Allen, 2018, EEF, 2019a).

Descriptor based assessments, taxonomies and matrices, like the Performing Arts skills matrix below can be used diagnostically by the teacher, or formatively and summatively by the teacher and pupils in giving explicit descriptors for specific levels, but the benefits can be limited (Figure 3.3) (Lindvall and Nitko, 1975, Christodoulou, 2016).

Skill	Level 1	Level 2	Level 3	Level 4	Level 5	Level 6
Practising	Understands what to do and repeats the work at least once more.	Repeats the work at least once, with some improvement in confidence.	Repeats the work, identifies problems, corrects them and improves.	Ability to work with little teacher input. Solves problems quickly and easily.	Ability to repeat work on own and as a part of a group, solving problems.	Minimal teacher involvement. Able to solve any problem set, on own or in a group.
Creating	Only uses examples set by teacher.	Some attempt to use a different idea to the one set.	Successful creation of a different idea using the set stimulus.	Imaginative creation of several ideas from the set stimulus.	Imaginative and stylish ideas from the set stimulus.	Both quality and quantity of ideas are excellent from the set stimulus.
Rehearsing	Can understand and play their part in a group piece repeatedly.	Can understand what everyone is doing and suggest improvements to the piece.	Can discuss, organise and practice their part as part of a whole group, helping others to improve.	Can discuss, organise and practice their own part and the whole piece as a whole group.	Shows a full understanding of their part and the piece and can lead their group in rehearsal.	Shows a full understanding of the work and uses time effectively and efficiently.
Performing	Can perform a simple part, with one or two breakdowns.	Can perform a simple part with focus and confidence.	Can perform a moderately difficult part with one or two breakdowns.	Can perform a moderately difficult part with some style and confidence.	Can perform a difficult part with one or two breakdowns.	Can perform a difficult part with style and confidence.
Evaluating	Can identify how much progress has been made with teacher prompts.	Can identify simply how much progress has been made.	Can identify, using some keywords, how much progress has been made and what work needs to be done.	Can identify, using keywords well, how themselves and others can improve at the tasks set.	Can identify using lots of keywords, how individuals and groups can improve at the tasks set.	Can identify, using all the keywords, how work has been, and can be completed by individuals and the whole class.
Audience Skills	Can listen to others.	Can listen quietly to others and applaud appropriately.	Can listen quietly, applaud appropriately and comment constructively on others work.	Can listen and applaud well, comment constructively and analyse critically, their own and others work.	Can listen quietly and comment on the success and weaknesses of their own and other pupils work.	Can listen and applaud well. Can comment critically about strengths and weaknesses of the work of the whole class.

Figure 3.3 Performing Arts Skills Matrix – Level Descriptors

Formative assessment or assessment for learning

Formative assessment creates information that helps drive learning and therefore progress forward (Bennett, 2011). With feedback, they are the most useful things a teacher can give to help improve pupil progress and goes to the heart of high-quality teaching. Unlike summative assessment, requiring teacher input at the start and end with pupil input in the middle, formative assessment has both teacher and pupil input integral to the ongoing assessment process (Wiliam, 2018). Formative assessment should be specific, frequent, repetitive and recorded as raw marks (MacCallum, 2000, DfE, 2013, Christodoulou, 2016).

Formative assessment, having no clear definition and therefore no clear evidence of its effectiveness, is wide open to (mis)interpretation (Bennett, 2011). This adds to Polesel et al.'s empirical evidence and Christodoulou's view that in recent years, assessment for learning hasn't been as effective as it could be. This has been due to the high stakes' accountability pressure from government insisting that assessment for learning be summative; moving from assessment *for* learning to assessment *of* learning (Polesel, 2014, Christodoulou, 2016).

Wiliam (2018) identifies five key strategies of formative assessment. They include:

1 Clarifying, sharing and understanding learning intentions and success criteria

2 Eliciting evidence of learning

3 Providing feedback that moves the learning forward

4 Activating learners as instructional resources for one another

5 Activating learners as owners of their own learning

Of course, formative assessment, like most other educational interventions, will not always work for all pupils, and not all studies find positive effects (Bennett, 2011). In order for it to have a positive impact, two conditions need to be met: First, pupils are given advice on how to improve; second, pupils act on that advice (Wiliam, 2018).

For a wealth of techniques and ideas related to formative assessment, see Dylan Wiliam's excellent book *Embedded Formative Assessment* (2018).

Marking and feedback

There is strong empirical evidence that feedback is an integral part of effective instruction in the classroom (Creemers, 1994) with marking as one form of feedback. What matters is not the "tick and flick" but giving feedback that helps a pupil improve and close any gaps (MacCallum, 2000, Hattie, 2012).

"Marking should ensure that action points are clear and require pupils themselves to take responsibility for solving a problem" (Ofsted, 2003). Interestingly, there is little quality evidence focused specifically on written marking. However, the research suggests that marking "needs to be manageable, meaningful and motivating" recommending that when marking tests, there should be a difference between marking *mistakes* and marking *misunderstandings*.

Marking is only valid when pupils have a chance to respond to it. Therefore, it is essential that pupils have "reflection time" or "Pupil Response" time in lessons (Ofsted, 2003). Ofsted previously noted that the marking of pupils' work was inconsistent (Ofsted, 2003). The recent inspection framework suggests that there is no need to deep mark (Ofsted, 2019b). The recommendation from research as to what there should be in pupils' books includes marking (grade + formative feedback) and spelling corrections (EEF, 2016).

Summative assessment or assessment of learning

Baseline assessments

Baseline assessments are the tests that are taken at the start and end of primary school and are important as they set the target grades, and therefore the trajectory against which pupil progress is measured, for the next five years (Nasen, 2014).

Summative assessments

Assessment *of* learning helps teachers identify where in the learning process a pupil is. Testing and exams offer the best form of summative assessment in being reliable and consistent and should be infrequent, standardised, set on a consistent scale and able to have shared meanings (Christodoulou, 2016).

Tests

Tests are good. Tests are useful. The use of low-stakes testing can contribute to progress in valuable ways (Ofsted, 2019a). Indeed, Barenberg, Roeder and Dutke (2018) state that the research shows strong evidence for the positive effects of testing.

However, in this age of performativity, testing can go too far. Assessment is gradually being defined as a test that is taught, rather than providing teaching that is tested, adding to teacher workload (Ofsted, 2017). As Dunford points out that while testing of itself is not a problem, the quality of the testing has become so narrow as to represent and measure little of what pupils know and can do.

> The curriculum should drive assessment, not the other way around; the assessment tail should not be wagging the curriculum dog.
>
> (Dunford, 2016)

Teachers usually test in three ways:

National tests – using past exam or test papers

Teachers use past exam or test papers to test pupils' knowledge and skills. The strengths of this approach include the validity and reliability of the test scores (national benchmark); best predictor of potential pupil grades; good practice for the pupils and its cheap. The limitations are that the papers may not cover exactly what the pupils have learnt and therefore need to be tailored.

Standardised tests – buying in standardised tests

Teachers use standardised tests from an outside provider to test pupil knowledge and skills. The strengths of this approach include the validity and reliability of the test scores (national benchmark), and sound predictor of potential pupil grades; digitalised responses provide a lot of data for parents and schools. The limitations are that the papers may not cover exactly what the pupils have learnt, can be expensive, but most importantly, these types of tests may be subject to a high degree of measurement error (Allen, 2018).

Create your own – creating your own assessments

Teachers create their own assessments to test pupil knowledge and skills. The strengths of this approach include the validity of the test scores in specifically assessing what pupils have learnt; it is cheap, especially if a bank of assessments already exist. The limitations are that it is not a sound predictor of potential pupil grades as there will be significant teacher bias in the questions being set, as a result the data will be unreliable.

As can be seen, there is a significant amount of scope for error and therefore making data invalid, unreliable or misrepresentative (Jones et al., 2017). Researchers have increasingly called for a framework (if there is no national or standardised testing) that can help schools more effectively define progress, and engage in a discussion as to the strengths and weaknesses of an assessment framework (EEF, 2019a).

Progress 8 and accountability

The government's current method of assessing a school's effectiveness is in its Progress 8 measure. So we are clear as to what it is:

> Progress 8 is designed to measure how well pupils progress between the end of primary and the end of secondary school. The score for each pupil is based on whether their actual GCSE scores are higher or lower than those achieved by pupils who had similar attainment at the end of primary school.
>
> (Andrews, 2017)

> Thus, Progress 8, after over 1500 years of education, rightly puts progress at the heart of how we measure a school, rather than pure attainment and is a major change in education (Paterson, 2013, Hattie, 2015, Andrews, 2017).

That's the good news.

However, with the introduction of Progress 8, schools have started seeing some negative effects emerging.

As an average measure, Progress 8 must have winners (above the average) and losers (below the average). Schools are continuing to "play the game", especially selective schools (Lenon, 2016, Cooper Gibson 2017, Gill, 2017, Andrews, 2018) by tailoring the curriculum they offer, especially in the humanities to improve their Progress 8 score (Polesel, Rice, and Dulfer, 2014, Gill, 2017, Andrews, 2018). As a result, there is confirmation that the curriculum in schools has narrowed (Biesta, 2008, Jones et al., 2017, Ofsted, 2019a) and that whilst the original intention of Progress 8 was to broaden the curriculum offer, the impact has been that the curriculum offer has reduced (Cooper Gibson, 2017).

Further, with Ofsted now signalling that they will only take account of national tests and not take a school's internal data into consideration (Ofsted, 2019b), means that school leaders are required to play the political game (Kelly, 2011), ensure their results are better than the value-added national average (positive Progress 8 score) which usually, mechanistically, will mean a "Good" or "Outstanding" Ofsted rating.

Other issues with Progress 8 include it being a zero-sum measure (only 50% of pupils can theoretically make progress); the ability to compare one school realistically with another and the so what? Factor. Data and Progress 8 performance tables tell us nothing about how to improve progress (Sherrington, 2018). Indeed, the research is clear that such value-added annual measures can be disingenuous.

First, where attendance in schools is good and a school's assessment system is rigorous and robust, the data is more likely to be reliable. But where attendance is less good (e.g., 10.9% of pupils were persistently absent in the autumn term of 2018 in the UK according to the Department for Education, DfE, 2019), means a significant number of pupils can be absent and unable to learn or be assessed.

In addition, with around 5% of pupils moving schools in the UK (Sharma, 2016), what's known as mobility, totals around 16% of pupils unable to be consistently present to learn or be assessed. This is before taking into consideration in-school factors affecting progress such as teacher variability.

Further, researchers have recently been able to demonstrate that genetic differences between pupils explain up to 20% of the variation in contextual value-added measures (Progress 8). These findings provide evidence that value-added measures of educational progress can be influenced by genetic differences between pupils, and therefore may provide a biased measure of school and teacher performance (Morris et al., 2018).

As a result, some researchers argue that whilst the best value-added models are a moderate predictor of how good a school is, due to variables such as instability (persistent school absence and mobility being part of these) and genetic difference, it would be wiser to judge schools over a two- or three-year period, rather than every year (van de Grift, 2009). As a result, researchers are increasingly clear that expected progress and the ability to measure progress in this way is a myth (Allen, 2018, Benyohai, 2018, Third Space Learning, 2019).

However, now that schools' internal assessments do not need to be inspected, there is an opportunity for schools to re-focus and concentrate on what happens in lessons; to re-group and re-energise their efforts on delivering a high-quality curriculum, taught as well as it can be with a balance of formative assessment to help drive progress and summative assessment to indicate how far pupils have travelled in their learning.

As regards the accountability of schools, much continues to change and quickly in national education policy. The volume of changes, range of changes and speed of changes are as significant as the changes themselves. Increased pressure and accountability from government and Ofsted are increasingly driving policy and practice in schools (Polesel, 2014, Dunford, 2016, Lenon, 2016), so much so that it is hard for teachers to separate external summative assessments from their internal formative assessments (EEF, 2019a).

Due to the high political pressure on schools to perform in summative testing and deliver what inspectors are looking for (Hanson, 2004, Kelly, 2011, Solomon, 2015), schools are highly focused on securing high performance in tests and exams to demonstrate how "on track" pupils are in the course of their school career (DfES, 2015) and therefore demonstrate their future success.

As a result, lessons have become formulaic and prescriptive, making teachers dependent on external assessments (Dunford, 2016). Hence, high stakes accountability is having a negative impact on teachers' creativity and experimentation with different strategies in the classroom (Ehren et al., 2015, Jones et al., 2017).

Looking back 15 years and Ofsted said in their review of assessment in 2003:

> In encouraging pupils to work for higher standards in tests and examinations, schools should focus on improving pupil's breadth and depth of subject understanding and skills, rather than concentrating too narrowly on the finer requirements of the next higher level or grade.
>
> (Ofsted, 2003)

This could have been written yesterday.

Finally, whilst the UK may be a lead player in the data game on the world stage (Kelly, 2011), we appear to have a school assessment system that has regressed 20 years by simply *measuring* (and according to Dunford, measuring little) pupil progress, not *improving* progress.

As a respected and competent country for data management, it appears to have little impact, with the PISA league tables (if we are doing league tables) ranking us 15th, behind Poland and Vietnam for education. Clearly, how we use data to improve learning, which hasn't improved in recent years (OECD, 2016), we need a radical shift back to improving progress in the classroom; back to improving formative assessment and back to improving teaching and learning.

> School leaders need to reclaim assessment as an essentially professional activity and match it to the curriculum needed by young people in the 21st century.
>
> (Dunford, 2016)

Summary

Progress

- Progress is concerned with learning more.

- Progress makes a difference to future job prospects, future income and is the measure of school effectiveness.

- Student progress is the yardstick by which teacher quality is assessed.

- There is no prescribed method of teaching. There are multiple definitions of learning. Our definition of progress in relation to teaching and learning is therefore unclear.

- Homework is a strong component of effective instruction and can make up to five months improvement in a student's progress.

- The curriculum taught is as important as the teaching of it to pupil progress.

- Having a scheme of work and programme of study is key to securing progress.

Learning and students

- Classrooms can have variation of up to four years between student abilities.

- Differentiating work by lowering expectations for some or setting different tasks for different groups or different learning styles does not improve progress.

- Questioning and feedback are key to developing learning.

- Learning cannot take place without the active engagement of every student with that strategy.

- Practice testing and distributed practice are effective in helping students learn.

- There is strong empirical evidence that feedback is an integral part of effective instruction in the classroom.

Teaching and teachers

- Teaching in the classroom is the single most important factor in school effectiveness.

- Variability in teacher quality can impede student progress by double the length of time or accelerate it by half the time.

- Improve the variation in teacher quality = improve progress.

- Formative assessment and coaching are particularly effective in helping teachers improve.

- Great teaching includes setting high expectations, giving high-quality instruction and remaining constantly challenging.

- Adapting teaching techniques and activities in a responsive way improves progress.

- The teacher in the classroom instigates the learning taking place with the best strategy.

Assessment

- Overall, the purpose of assessment is to improve standards, not merely to measure them.

- Diagnostic assessment is little used, under-researched, a central aspect to effective teaching around the world and important.

- Formative assessment creates information that helps drive learning and therefore progress forward.

- Marking is only valid when students have a chance to respond to it. Therefore, it is essential that students have "reflection time" or "Pupil Response" time in lessons.

- The use of low-stakes testing can contribute to progress in valuable ways. Research shows strong evidence for the positive effects of testing.

- Progress 8 puts progress at the heart of how we measure a school. However, researchers are increasingly clear that expected progress and the ability to measure progress in this way is a myth.

4 Progress over time: step-by-step success

Progress over time plain and simple:

Progress in learning that takes place over
a key stage (a curriculum map), a year
(a programme of study), a set of lessons
(a scheme of work) or a lesson.

In this chapter, we will cover:

- What we mean by progress over time
- Curriculum maps, programmes of study and schemes of work
- The importance of clarity, comprehensiveness and coherence
- Tracking sheets

Introduction

Having a clearer definition of progress and a clearer understanding as to what the research says about progress, we can start to make our way towards the classroom. But just before we go in, we also need to be clear about how all of those small, incremental steps of progress in the classroom fit together in the educational journey; progress over time (Figure 4.1).

Like any journey, it is important to have a map. A visual tool to help summarise and visualise the journey from where you are at this moment in time to your destination. This summary of the journey you are taking can also give an estimation of how long the journey will take, with an idea of what you are likely to experience along the way.

As in life, so it is with learning.

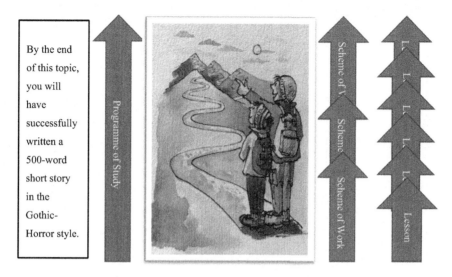

Figure 4.1 Progress over Time: Guiding Step-by-Step Success

In school, learning, the inner educational journey that takes place there, is made explicit and mapped out through a curriculum map (an overview of what is taught in every subject, in every year group, over the year), a programme of study (a more detailed guide as to what will be studied in each year group, in each subject over the year) and a scheme of work (what will be studied in each year group, in each subject, lesson-by-lesson over a half term or topic). These documents are the very foundation of learning in the classroom and as such are the bedrock of progress. In my experience, the success or failure in ensuring every child achieves their potential is rooted in the presence and application of (or lack of) these documents.

No one would ever consider setting out on a journey without a map of how to get there. Similarly, no school and no teacher can teach and ensure the pupil is making sufficient progress without these educational maps.

What follows is a brief overview of what these documents are, what they are used for and how they contribute to the successful progress of the pupil.

Progress over a year or key stage and across the school – curriculum maps

A curriculum map enables the reader to see at a glance what topics are being taught across subjects in a particular year group at a particular time. It is particularly useful to see what skills and knowledge are being taught *concurrently* in different subjects and therefore speed up progress in lessons through offering the teachers the possibility of supporting each other's lessons and reinforcing what is being learnt.

For example, in Figure 4.2, Year 8 in Art (War and Art through Cubism), Dance (Guernica) and History (The Hundred Years' War) are studying three subjects

YEAR 8	Autumn 1	Autumn 2	Spring 1	Spring 2	Summer 1	Summer 2
English	*Frankenstein:* Imaginative writing	*Frankenstein:* Imaginative writing	American Literature:*Of Mice and Men*	The Tempest: persuasive writing	The Tempest: persuasive writing	Conflict Poetry
Maths	Proportional reasoning	Representations using graphs	Algebraic techniques	Developing number	Developing geometry	Reasoning with data
Science	Ecosystem processes	Metals and acids; Foods and fuels	Health and lifestyle	The periodic table; Motion and pressure	Electricity and magnetism	Adaptations and inheritance; Separation / Earth
Art	Still Life: Drawing with Watercolour	Still Life: In style of Matisse / Cezanne.	War in Art: Cubism & Picasso	War in Art: Vorticism & Camouflage	Large chalk and charcoal drawings	Working with digital photography,
Computer Science	E-Safety + Keeping data safe	Algorithms and Programming /Pseudocode	Data Representation	Outcome to produce own	Code.org E	Pashed
Dance	Slavery	Capoeira	Feelings through dance based on Guernica	Swansong	Ghost Dances	Street Dance
Drama	Othello	The Terrible Fate of Humpy Dumpty	Anne Frank	Physical Theatre	Shaun's Story	Our Day Out
DT	Drawing skills, Workshop safety	Manufacturing tools and equipment	Design briefs and specifications (Granny bag)	Drawing skills, Workshop safety	Manufacturing tools and equipment	Design briefs and specifications (Granny bag)
French	School life	School life	Leisure	Leisure	Where I live	Where I live
Geography	Population and Migration	Biomes	The North/South Divide	The North/South Divide	Coastal Environments	Global Superpowers
History	Ancient Civilisations	Ancient Civilisations	The Hundred Years' War	The Renaissance	The Slave Trade (British)	The British Empire
Music	Reggae	Fanfares	Rap	Blues	Indian Music	Performance Project
PSHE	Internet Safety & Extremism/ Radicalisation	SRE	Managing Personal Finance	Careers	Personal Development/ Behaviour	Careers & Finance
RE	What does it mean to be a Christian?	What does it mean to be a Muslim?	Importance of revelation in religions?	The problem of evil and suffering	Comparing Abrahamic faiths	Religion and the News
Spanish	How were your vacations? Using past tense	Socializing and leisure time	Talking about school	Talking about food	Making arrangements	Describing your town or village
Sport & Nutrition	Netball Badminton Athletics	Football Handball Athletics	Badminton Football Athletics	Handball Basketball Athletics	Hockey Cricket Athletics	Cricket Netball Athletics

Figure 4.2 Example of a Year 8 Curriculum Map

related to war at the start of the spring term. These subjects could therefore plan and ensure they reinforce shared key concepts, themes and vocabulary.

Alternatively, it may be useful to use a curriculum map to see what is being taught sequentially to build on previously learnt skills and knowledge and speed up progress as a result. For example, in Figure 4.2, Year 8 in the summer term in English are studying conflict poetry. Here, the teacher can draw on the previously learnt knowledge of the class from their lessons in Art, Dance and History which they learnt at the start of the spring term.

This not only helps potentially speed up progress in English in this topic by drawing on previous learning but also helps pupils remember and recall the information related to the other subjects.

Any curriculum map should be checked for being clear, comprehensive and coherent.

> Thus, a curriculum map is a thematic guide to the curriculum and what will be taught throughout the school. It will not tell you what will be taught lesson by lesson, nor what the learning aims and outcomes are. It is simply an overview as to what will be taught.

Clear

- Is the outcome for each topic clear?

- Are the skills and knowledge being learnt in each topic clear?

Comprehensive

- Does every subject teach everything that is required by law?

- Does every subject teach everything that is required by the exam boards?

Coherent

- Do any topics support subsequent topics for each subject (sequential coherence)?

- Do any topics support similar topics at that time in other subjects (concurrent coherence)?

- Can any topics be studied at another time of the year and be more effective (more coherent) as a result?

Progress over a year across a subject – programmes of study

In order to make progress in learning, we need to know where we are progressing to. We need a destination. We need clarity over what we are going to achieve. As well as the *map* to help us *get* to our destination, we also need a *schedule*, so that we know we are going to reach our destination *on time* and with plenty of time to spare.

This is a programme of study.

A few key points about a programme of study:

> - A programme of study determines the *pace* of the curriculum and ensures that *everything that should be taught is taught.*
>
> - As far as possible, it maps out *when* all topics and skills are taught taking into consideration holidays and key school events.
>
> - A programme of study is not a scheme of work. It is the foundation for a scheme of work.
>
> - A programme of study details *when* a topic is to be studied. A scheme of work details *what* is going to be studied in detail each lesson.
>
> - A programme of study drives the *pace* of progress in learning.
>
> - The scheme of work provides the *milestones* for that progress.

Thus, as can be seen from an example of a Maths programme of study for the Autumn term in Year 11 (Figure 4.3), a programme of study maps the curriculum in terms of the exam specification, topics, homework and assessment against time in terms of the lessons in a week and the weeks in the school year. In this way, teachers, school leaders, governors and parents can be assured that the curriculum, if taught and learnt effectively, will be completely covered in good time.

PROGRAMME OF STUDY – EXAMPLE -YEAR 11						
Week	Dates	Wk A/B	Lesson	Specification Content	Unit / Topic / Paper	Independent / Homework Tasks
0	28/08/2019	NO TEACHING				
1	02/09/2019	A	1	N11	Number	Complete exercises on N11-N12
			2	N11	Number	
			3	N12	Number	
2	09/09/2019	B	1	N12	Number	Complete exercises on N13-N14
			2	N13	Number	
			3	N13	Number	
			4	N14	Number	
3	15/09/2019	A	1	N14	Number	Complete exercises on N15-N16
			2	N15	Number	
			3	N15	Number	
4	23/09/2019	B	1	N16	Number	Revise N1-N16
			2	N16	Number	
			3	Number Test	Number	
			4	Number Evaluation	Number	
5	30/09/2019	A	1	A16	Algebra	Complete exercises on A16-A17
			2	A16	Algebra	
			3	A17	Algebra	
6	07/10/2019	B	1	A17	Algebra	Complete exercises on A17-A18
			2	A18	Algebra	
			3	A18	Algebra	
			4	A19	Algebra	
7	14/10/2019	A	1	A19	Algebra	Complete exercises on A19-A20
			2	A20	Algebra	
			3	A20	Algebra	
HALF TERM BREAK						

Figure 4.3 Example of a Programme of Study – Autumn Half Term

Similar to a curriculum map, any programme of study should be checked for being clear, comprehensive and coherent.

Clear

- Is the outcome for each programme of study clear?

- Is the curriculum content and timing for each topic clear?

- Are the skills and knowledge being developed through the programmes of study clear?

- Is the curriculum being learnt in lessons, through homework and the assessment timings clear?

Comprehensive

- Is all the curriculum that is required by law being taught?

- Is all the curriculum that is required by the exam boards being taught?

Coherent

- Does each topic support subsequent topics for each year group (sequential coherence)?

- Can any topics be studied at another time of the year and be more effective (more coherent) as a result?

The programme of study then supports progress in lessons in the following ways:

1 *Pace*: Results between topics, between pupils or between classes are more likely to be higher and consistent if there are consistent programmes of study in place in a department and in a school. It is essential that there is a centralised format of the programme of study so that there is consistency of delivery across a school.

2 *Structured supportive learning*: Opportunities are created for the curriculum (sequential coherence) and other subjects (concurrent coherence) to support the learning taking place. As a result, progress is likely to be higher as previous learning is developed further or current learning is reinforced.

3 *Empowering*: Ensuring a programme of study is fit for purpose and to a high standard, empowers teachers and middle leaders and provides them with the focus and significant support to help them drive their lessons and their courses more effectively, ensuring they are completed successfully.

4 *Key to progress*: If there are issues with progress to address, the sooner the programme of study is discounted as an issue, the sooner the school can move on

to explore other issues to address and resolve. Having a clear, comprehensive and coherent programme of study in place from the start removes the possibility of this being a potential issue.

5 ***Confidence in the school***: Having programmes of study in place reassures teachers, pupils, leaders, parents and governors that what should be taught is being taught.

Progress over a half a term in a subject – schemes of work

A scheme of work outlines the learning that takes place over a topic, usually each half term, lesson by lesson. What's often not clear in a scheme of work is its aim. How will pupils know they have successfully completed their studies in this topic? For example, "By the end of this topic, you will have successfully written a 500-word short story in the Gothic-Horror style".

This is important as it enables the pupils to see the point of the scheme of work and position it in relation to other learning that has taken place previously and is taking place currently. The end goal also helps contextualise the learning that will be taking place through the scheme of work, giving meaning to all the classwork and homework covered in the subject in the following weeks.

> A scheme of work is a series of lessons that are delivered sequentially so that each lesson stands on the shoulders and further develops the learning from previous lessons, culminating in a final test, presentation or assessment.

Each lesson has a clear goal, presented as a learning objective, set of learning outcomes or posed as a question. The scheme of work also includes the activities, assessments and homework that are needed to successfully achieve the final goal. Figure 4.4 is an example of a scheme of work.

As with the curriculum map and the programme of study, this is another opportunity for the school to ensure that the curriculum is delivered in a clear, comprehensive and coherent way.

Clear

- Is the outcome for the scheme of work clear?

- Are the skills and knowledge being developed by the scheme of work clear?

- Is the differentiation for different abilities clear?

A huge amount has been written about differentiation, beyond the scope of this juncture in the book and this book. Suffice to say that differentiation in relation to

MUSIC	Year 8 - Blues	Overall goal: Group Performance of a 12 Bar Blues Song			SPRING 1
Week	National Curriculum KS3 Strategy Skills	Learning Objectives / Activities	Resources	Differentiated Learning & Outcomes	Homework / Assessment
1	Controlling sounds Singing Playing together Improvising Reading Practising Rehearsing Listening	Listen to / Sing "I feel good" Understand timing of words with 12 bar blues (12BB). Fit improvised fills with the words. Play a Q and A tune using the blues scale, alongside the 12 BB.	Song sheets Backing track Keyboards	Be able to play the 12BB and / or the blues scale, group / solo, one / both hands & play Q & A tune in a stylish way.	Test – 12 Bar Blues and notes of the Blues Scale.
2	Controlling sounds Composing Playing together Improvising Reading Practising Rehearsing Listening	Sing / play a Q and A tune using the blues scale, alongside the 12 BB, at least twice through, with an introduction and ending. Understand the notes of the Blues Scale, Improvisation and the chords in the 12 BB. Programme the keyboard to a suitable backing beat, with an introduction and ending.	Manuscript Backing track Keyboards	Be able to play the 12BB, blues scale, group / solo, one / both hands and one idea for a beginning and ending of a song with a suitable intro & ending.	Write out the meanings of the following words: Introduction, Coda, Fill, Improvisation, Walking Bass, Syncopation, Sharp, Flat, Question and Answer, Call and Response.
3	Controlling sounds Singing Playing together Improvising Reading Practising Rehearsing Listening	Sing "Rock Around the Clock". Understand how the words fit with 12BB. Understand how the Instrumental fits with the words. Begin work on preparing a Blues song using Improvisation, a regular tune and all the keyboard facilities. Add instrumental part.	Song sheets Backing track Keyboards	Understand what an instrumental is and know what part they are to play in their group piece, including a sustained improvisation.	Write out on Manuscript paper the twelve - bar blues, the blues scale, C major and C minor scales.
4	Controlling sounds Composing Singing Playing together Improvising Reading Practising Rehearsing Listening	Understand stages of Composition – Explore, Select, Structure, Revise. Performance – Practice, Rehearse, Perform. Continue work in groups on Blues piece. Include walking bass, tune, chords, backing beat, introduction and ending. Understand what work is needed to improve and finish the piece next lesson.	Song sheets Backing track Keyboards	Understand their part in the piece and what and when they should play, have practiced their parts and be rehearsing the whole piece.	Find out and write a biography of ONE of the following Blues musicians – John Lee Hooker, Bessie Smith or Muddy Waters.
5	Controlling sounds Composing Singing Playing together Improvising Reading Practising Rehearsing Listening	Recap Understanding of stages of Composition – Explore, Select, Structure, Revise. Performance – Practice, Rehearse, Perform. All pieces to be completed and have the required sections. – Introduction, Backing Beat, Fills, Tune, Improvisation, Walking Bass, Chords, Twelve Bar Blues, Blues Scale and an Ending..	Song sheets Backing track Keyboards	Rehearse the pieces and prepare for a performance. Play their part in time as well as have incorporated improvisation into their piece.	Prepare for final performance next lesson. Spelling test.
6	Controlling sounds Composing Singing Playing together Improvising Reading Rehearsing Listening Performing	Be able to perform their blues piece in an organised and professional way. Be able to be a good audience. Evaluation of the performance Be able to identify and discuss the strengths and areas for development of individual and class performance of their songs.	Song sheets Backing track Keyboards Video camera	Presentation and performance of Blues song. Give a strong, convincing and confident performance of their piece.	Revise all work for an end of term test.

Figure 4.4 Music Year 8 Blues Scheme of Work (Spring Term)

a scheme of work is the understanding that a teacher sets up a lesson not only so that every pupil can access it but also be challenged by it.

It should be clear in any scheme of work how the activities are differentiated, so that all pupils can access the lesson and all pupils can achieve or exceed the standard of work of which they are aiming to achieve.

Comprehensive

- Do the lessons and homework teach everything that is required?

- Do the lessons and homework enable every pupil to achieve at and beyond their expected ability (i.e. sufficiently differentiated)?

- Do the assessments sufficiently assess the skills and knowledge being learnt?

Coherent

- Are the lessons ordered in the most logical way (sequential coherence)?

- How does this topic support other topics and other subjects being learnt (concurrent coherence)?

For example, and just to show you what is meant by coherence, let's have a go at constructing a scheme of work. So, the topic the pupils need to learn is about castles. They need to understand the whole background to castles, why they were built where they were and what their importance was. Here are the topics:

1 Castles today – what's the difference?

2 Castles – why some survived and others didn't?

3 Great castles in history

4 Making a castle – problems and solutions

5 What makes a castle a castle?

6 Why build a castle?

In what order would you put them? What would your justification be for that order?

For example, you might have chosen to put them in order of the *chronological development* of castles (i.e. the logic behind the development of castles over time), one could structure the topics as follows:

1 What makes a castle a castle?

2 Why build a castle there?

3 Making a castle – problems and solutions

4 Great castles in history – what's the difference?

5 Castles – why some survived and others didn't?

6 Castles today

In which order did you put them? Whenever I have done this exercise with teachers or school leaders, even though there are only six topics to re-arrange, everyone has come up with a different order. The point here is two-fold.

First, there is no specific formula for writing an effective scheme of work. Second, as long as there is an intellectual coherence behind the order (and there are many) and the pupils understand the meaning behind that order, will help them learn and make better progress as a result.

Progress in books

To summarise, all the above should be evident in pupils' books and files.

- A tracker sheet should ideally show higher test scores and harder (higher) grades being achieved over time.

- Assessment grades should be the same or higher in relation to target grades.

- Progress should be able to be seen by comparing the work completed at the start of a book (simpler, shorter, less accurate) to the work completed at the end of a book (longer, harder, more accurate).

- Progress can be shown by comparing the work completed at the start of a topic (simpler, shorter, less accurate) to that at the end of a topic (longer, harder, more accurate).

Summary

- A curriculum map is a thematic guide to the curriculum and what will be taught throughout the school.

- A programme of study determines the pace of the curriculum and ensures that everything that should be taught is taught.

- A programme of study drives the *pace* of progress in learning.

- A scheme of work is a series of lessons that are delivered sequentially so that each lesson stands on the shoulders and further develops the previous lessons, culminating in a final test, presentation or assessment.

- No school and no teacher can teach and ensure the pupil is learning effectively without a scheme of work and programme of study being in place and followed.

- Books should have a completed tracker sheet, with assessment grades that are the same or higher in relation to target grades; work completed at the start of a book is simpler, shorter, less accurate compared to the work completed at the end of a book which should be longer, harder and more accurate.

Progress: in and beyond the classroom

Progress in and beyond the classroom: a Credo

Being clearer about progress over time and how lessons fit into a scheme of work and programme of study, it is now time to enter the classroom and look at the micro-skills of teaching that secure the incremental changes and demonstrate progress in learning. In response to Biesta's article (2008) and in the style of John Dewey's Pedagogic Creed (1897), I am offering a current perspective on what I believe is the purpose of education in helping pupils learn about themselves and the outside world in which they live (Illeris, 2007).

I believe pupils need to learn a set of basic skills, without which they will find life in society difficult. In addition, they need to identify and develop a set of skills, of talents, that are specific to them, so each pupil can find their own place in and make their unique contribution to society. Hence, I believe education is first and foremost about educating young people to be more skilled, enabled and empowered.

A close second to learning skills I believe is for pupils to also have a bank of knowledge that supports and strengthens those skills. Hence, I believe education is also about ensuring young people know more about the world in which they live and are able to function successfully within it as a result.

I believe both skills and knowledge are enhanced by a young person's ability to be accurate and precise, and to know what is right *and* wrong, better or worse. Hence, there is a place in education for teaching pupils how to be accurate and precise in what they do.

And life is full of challenges. Educating pupils in how to face and manage challenge is a life lesson in itself. Hence, I believe that educating pupils and helping them learn how to be more resilient in the face of adversity is central to education and the student's preparation for adult life.

Finally, I believe the mark of a successful upbringing, the mark of a successful education is in every child's ability to fly the nest and make their own way successfully in the world, independent of their parents or their school. Hence, my final perspective on progress in education lies in the pupil learning how to be successful and independent.

This section offers teachers and leaders deliberate strategies to ensure there is "cognitive change" in the pupils (Hattie, 2012, p.16). Chapters 5 to 9 are aimed primarily at teachers as they have the biggest educational interaction with pupils. These chapters focus specifically on developing progress in skills, knowledge, accuracy, resilience and independent learning in the classroom. Chapters 10–12 are aimed more towards teachers and school leaders in looking at progress across the school through the lenses of assessment, school leadership and school evaluation.

The section concludes with suggested websites and books that take further the points raised in this book.

5 Progress in the lesson: skills

Progress in skills plain and simple:

Progress in a skill pertains to see increases in the pupil being more skilful in what they do.

The first, and arguably most important measure of progress in a lesson, is skill.

In this chapter, we will cover:

- What we mean by skill
- Consciously teaching skills
- Enabling pupils to be more skilful
- Modelling skills
- Teaching skills in practice: activities and strategies
- Implications for leaders on skills
- Questions to help further understand and improve skills

Introduction

The first measure of progress in the classroom to discuss is skill, for example, to be able to write.

The first, and arguably most important, measure of progress in a lesson is the pupils' ability to demonstrate improvements in the skills related to that particular subject (EEF, 2019d). This chapter concentrates on the pupil's ability to demonstrate that they are more skilled in something at the end of a lesson or scheme of work than they were at the start. Teaching skills is where there are the greatest differences between subjects. It is therefore important that teachers should be aware of the specific skills they are teaching that can only be taught in their subject, and the skills that are taught and in common with other subject areas.

The focus of this chapter is to demonstrate the progress in learning related to skills. This is the incremental increase in the difficulty of a pupil's subject-specific skills; understanding and being able to demonstrate increasingly difficult work, work that is harder, more complex, more challenging in its difficulty resulting in the increase in the pupil's ability to master it.

Thus, in the classroom, when teaching a skill, it is important that pupils understand what the teacher is asking them to do and how it will help them in their education, and in life, to be able to do it. In addition, it's important to teach pupils not just how to do something that becomes increasingly more difficult, but why they need to be able to do it.

What we mean by progress in skills

MEASURE OF PROGRESS: THE DIFFICULTY OF A SKILL

FROM THE TEACHER	FROM THE PUPIL
INCREASINGLY DIFFICULT ACTIVITIES	INCREASING MASTERY / ABILITY
MODELLING SKILLS	KNOWLEDGE OF WHAT TO DO
EXPLAINING SKILLS	KNOWLEDGE OF HOW TO DO IT
FEEDBACK	MORE ABLE TO DO IT

So, what do we mean by progress in a skill? Having a skill is the ability to do something well, to be able to demonstrate an expertise in something. Therefore, the first measure of progress is the degree to which a pupil demonstrates a progressively more difficult skill. It is an active, demonstrable measure.

Something is harder, more complex. This requires a teacher to model, explain and demonstrate to the pupils as to what defines the difficulty or complexity of the skill being learnt. This requires a specific teaching technique.

An example would be a pupil learning to play the piano. Here, the pupil must learn to use the right part of the body to contact the correct part of an instrument in the correct way, so that a sound is produced. This must be repeated, with slight variations, so the pupil can correctly play a multiple number of notes (sounds) in the right way before any music can be created.

For musicians, scientists, sportsmen and women, dancers, actors, chefs, computer scientists, carpenters and metal workers, all must be able to understand the external kinaesthetic process of making something physically work in order to then make progress in a skill. In Mathematics, English, Modern Foreign Languages, and the Humanities, it is in the pupils' ability to understand increasingly complex or difficult concepts and theories that need to be understood first, which underpin a skill.

The success criteria, how we know a skill has been learnt, can be demonstrated in the increase in a pupil's grades (increasing in difficulty) over time. Pupils should achieve a successively higher score in any tests over time to demonstrate the increased mastery of increasingly difficult topics and increasingly harder skills.

What the research says about the teaching and learning of skills

The teaching and learning of skills have the most writing and research on them in the available educational literature. Most people and most authors view "progress" as the progress of a pupil's skill.

In addition to what the research says about progress in general as outlined in Chapter 3, there are a couple of additional points raised specifically about progress related to skills.

Skills are best taught through modelling (Muijs and Reynolds, 2017) as well as combining basic skills with more complex thinking skills, recognising that the skills pupils need for the 21st century include the ability to think creatively and to evaluate and analyse information. Further, rather than creating more knowledge tests, there is a need for tests that measure more of the skills pupils' need to succeed today (Silva, 2008). This includes schools working more closely with employers, and teachers being more up-to-date in an increasingly technological world (UKCES, 2014).

There is broad agreement that skills, alongside knowledge and accuracy, are intertwined and are the "warp and weft" of every lesson, in every school, every day (Dunford, 2016, p.66, Kirby, 2016, p.16). There is also recognition that skills are developed in two ways – directly and indirectly (Christodoulou, 2016, p.23).

However, there is some lack of clarity as to whether we need to develop skills, not just knowledge (Dunford, 2016, p.64), or knowledge, not just skills (Kirby, 2015, p.18). Either way, skills are central to the teaching and learning process.

Consciously teaching skills: how skills are taught

There are several ways that teachers can explicitly teach skills which are discussed in more detail below.

Iterative progress: gradually increasing the challenge

With any new topic, starting things simply and increasing the difficulty as the lesson or the scheme of work progresses, is how most teachers structure progress in skills. The logic here being straight forward; there are a set of skills which need to be mastered first before more difficult or more complex skills, and learning can take place.

This would be the equivalent of starting teaching in the shallow end of a swimming pool and gradually teaching the pupils to swim successfully at the deep end. This structure works well as a staged approach to learning. The risk, however, is that those who can learn quickly or who are more talented in this area may get bored very quickly.

Thus, there is a need to ensure there are differentiated activities, additional work, stretch and super stretch activities available so that every pupil is working at their level of ability, whilst the few that need the additional support can be supported with no loss of progress for the many.

Immersive progress: scaffolding the challenge

On the other hand, and a method which can secure far more progress in lessons, is to turn the challenge the other way around; we start at the deep end. The logic here is that there are a set of skills that need to be mastered but not necessarily in a set order. This structure works well in quickly teaching the necessary skills, allowing the more talented or faster learners to learn at their own pace, allowing the teacher to support and "scaffold" the learning, so the pupils who are struggling are provided with additional support.

The risk here is that the skills, and the ability to learn those skills in a lesson is just too complex, too inaccessible for most pupils, and as a result, most of the class struggle rather than swim. Therefore, this approach works more effectively later in a topic, later in the year, or with older pupils when pupils are likely to be more skilled and therefore more likely to cope with the high level of challenge from the very start.

Introducing a skill: modelling and classroom visualisers

This is the most common method by which teachers teach pupils a skill and that is by modelling it for them. "Copy what I do". This is fine when either the skills being taught are explicit, less fine when they are not. Making learning explicit helps pupils see what needs to be learnt and as a result more easily and effectively know what to do. It is therefore important that the teacher, when modelling a skill for the pupils, makes it as explicit as possible, for example, for only about £40 each, the teacher can use a camera or classroom visualiser to help demonstrate the writing or drawing skills in pupils' books on the board.

Explaining a skill: teach them how to do it

Once a pupil grasps the basics, the teacher can then begin to get the pupils to practice the skill themselves. "See how it's done. Try this yourself". This is the moment the pupils metaphorically get into the water to swim. It is therefore important at this stage that the teacher provides clarity of explanation and reassurance that all will be well.

Having a simple and user-friendly way of seeing/hearing how well pupils are trying out a new skill is essential for the teacher to quickly ascertain how effectively they have taught, and how effectively the pupils have learnt, the lesson.

Feedback on a skill: coach skill not luck!

Once pupils have grasped a skill, confidence through practice is necessary. "Show me that was skill and not luck!" is a phrase I often use with pupils at this stage in their learning as the fledgling skill emerges and pupils need encouragement to keep trying this new skill and develop their confidence in it further.

It is important here that the teacher, when coaching and feeding back to the pupil, can correct any misunderstandings and feedback as specifically as possible how well pupils are progressing. Pupils who have mastered this part of the lesson can be used to support the teacher as junior coaches and check, support and give feedback to other pupils on behalf of the teacher.

Checking the progress in learning: effective questioning

Whichever way a teacher teaches a skill, their use of questioning the pupils, collectively or individually, is an important tool in the teacher's toolbox. Hearing explicitly how well the pupils have understood and learnt what has been taught, through effective questioning, is key. Using thumbs up, or a green card (I understand and am confident in what I am doing), or thumbs down, or a red card (I don't understand, or am not confident in what I am doing) will be helpful and efficient ways for the teacher to ascertain through their questioning, the level of skills development in the class.

Activities and strategies that promote progress in skills

What follows in this chapter are a collection of recommended strategies and activities that, when used and applied well in lessons, will help demonstrate progress related to skills. Interspersed with these strategies and activities are examples of progress in skills either from my own or others' professional experience.

Using and applying all the suggested strategies and activities may ensure amazing progress in lessons; however, that is not the intention here. These sections in this and each of the next four chapters offer a range of strategies and activities that should be used when the situation requires. *It is therefore required for the teacher to use their professional judgement to decide which is the best time to apply them.*

The strategies and activities are in a suggested succedent order; the strategies and activities at the start being recommended for use at the start of the lesson or topic and those at the end, useful at the end of a lesson or topic.

Many of the strategies and activities may not be new to the reader. However, the value of each strategy lies in promoting progress in a particular area and suggesting a timing when the strategy or activity is likely to be most effective.

For experienced teachers, this section provides several recommendations which may be used to refresh the memory of strategies and activities used in the past and are maybe needed to be brought back to the fore. The strategies and activities will also provide confirmation that already doing these strategies and activities with your classes confirms the good practice in your choice of teaching strategies.

For less experienced teachers, I hope you find this section useful and full of easy-to-apply ideas that will help you and your classes experience far more progress being made in a shorter duration of time with respect to the students' skills.

Enjoy!

STRATEGY 5.1: The skills matrix

I have used this strategy for years and shared it with other departments and other schools. It is brilliant for making the skills to be learnt and standards expected explicit to the pupils.

Outcome

The pupils have a very clear understanding of what skills are being learnt over the course of their studies and the trajectory of difficulty of the skills being learnt.

Use of the strategy: at the start, middle and end of a topic

This strategy is useful throughout a topic or key stage, so pupils have a clear reference point in any lesson, at any point, as required. It clearly states the skills and the development of those skills that will happen during a lesson, over the time of a topic or in the scheme of work.

A useful strategy for also developing: accuracy and independent learning.

Resources

The skills matrix on A4 or A3 paper for display (see Figure 7 on p.38, as an example).

Continued on next page

How it works

▉ Key skills that are being taught in a subject (e.g. in Music, Dance and Drama = the ability to practice, rehearse, perform, create, listen and evaluate) are displayed with the expectation expressed for each level of the skill (e.g. Levels 1–9).

▉ This is displayed, taking up a whole display board, permanently there as a reference point for the teacher and pupils when discussing expectations, skills assessment and evaluation and therefore the progress of those skills.

How will the teacher ensure learning has taken place?

Through questioning pupils and ensuring the pupils can accurately recognise in real life the features described on the matrix, able to evaluate them and describe the features accurately and independently.

How will progress be seen to be made?

Progress in this activity will be visible through pupils clearly both demonstrating and being able to independently and accurately evaluate skills against the matrix descriptors.

STRATEGY 5.2: The skills tracker sheet

This strategy is a powerful learning tool in helping pupils understand how their skills are to be developed with the bonus of ticking off those skills as they are mastered over the year.

Outcome

Pupils have a very clear understanding of what skills they are learning through the tracking sheets making the skills being taught over the year, and the expectations they need to reach, explicit.

Use of the strategy: at the start and the end of a topic

This strategy is useful over a year, so pupils have a clear reference point in any lesson, at any point, as required. It clearly states the skills to be covered over the time of a topic or in the scheme of work. This enables the pupil to clearly see what skill is being learnt and the order of topics, so the logic and scaffolded nature of the scheme of work is clear to the pupils. It clarifies what the pupils need to do to develop and master those skills.

A useful strategy for also developing: knowledge and resilience.

Continued on next page

Resources

A tracking sheet on A5 paper to be put in pupils' books.

How it works

■ Target grades and key skills that are being taught in a subject are specified on a tracking sheet as column headings with the topics being taught (and the relevant skills being mastered in that topic) as row headings.

■ A5 size allows a sheet to be put in the front of a pupil's book and used permanently as a reference point when discussing expectations, skills assessment and the progress of those skills.

How will the teacher ensure learning has taken place?

Through questioning pupils and providing opportunities for the pupils to accurately explain how they have developed their skills and exceeded/met/not met the expected grades.

How will progress be seen to be made?

Progress in this activity will be visible through pupils clearly both demonstrating and being able to accurately evaluate their own skills against the target grades.

STRATEGY 5.3: Teaching a master class

This is how I wish every lesson was with pupils. In this lesson, the teacher is delivering a master class with the pupils. The delivery is not learning about music, it's about being musicians together and learning music. It's not learning about Science, it's about being scientists together and learning science. The teacher is the skilled craftsman and helping pupils be more skilled at their craft.

Outcome

By the end of the lesson, the pupil is more skilled than they were at the beginning.

Use of the strategy: at the start or end of a topic

This strategy is particularly useful at the start or end of a topic. It gets the pupils into a positive mindset that they are being treated as young professionals

Continued on next page

with the high expectations and work ethic that entails. This strategy is useful towards the end of a topic in taking the quality of work that the pupils have produced to the next level.

A useful strategy for also developing: knowledge and independent learning.

Resources

As required.

How it works

▣ The teacher sets the high expectations that pupils are to work on a higher level as young professionals and approach the lesson as a master class.

▣ The teacher models and demonstrates high-level skills which are to be developed and improved and coaches the pupils in improving them.

▣ Pupils are expected to demonstrate high-quality questioning and complete ability to work independently.

How will the teacher ensure learning has taken place?

Through modelling the high expectations and the high level of work expected. Through the high level of challenge and the level of coaching to secure pupils achieve and meet those high expectations.

How will progress be seen to be made?

The measure of success is in the high expectations being met, with clear development of a skill between the start and the end of a lesson/topic by the pupil, and seeing a pupil being increasingly skilled, knowledgeable and more able to independently develop that skill.

PROGRESS IN PRACTICE: lessons learnt in skills – the master class

Ben was a football coach at one of the schools in which I worked. As a football coach, he wanted to teach and pass on his passion, knowledge and skills in football to a group of like-minded, skilled and enthusiastic pupils.

Continued on next page

I'm sure that the story is one that is seen regularly across the country – of football teams' winning. School trophy cabinets are full of the brash but celebratory souvenirs of this. However, his work with the boys' and girls' football teams was particularly successful, with both teams winning their respective leagues in a very short space of time. As a measure of progress, this success was exceptional and illustrates well the cumulative progress in practice; the daily iterative excellence of a master class in sport.

Through high challenge, clear goals, incremental challenges that increased in complexity and difficulty every lesson, supported by personalised feedback, the pupils increased and developed their skills to the point that they were quickly the best in their league. This was done by a carefully thought through programme that covered everything and was executed in a user-friendly and personalised way for every pupil. That a large number of pupils from the senior teams then had the opportunity to study abroad was an additional validation of the level of skills achieved and attained by the pupils.

With regard to progress, the clear focus was on the development and improvement of the pupils' footballing skills through the difficulty and mastery of the challenges set by the teacher. In addition, there was also the necessity that the whole process should be time sensitive. Teachers must be aware of the time in which they must deliver the curriculum they need to teach and manage that time for the pupils as effectively as possible. This example works well in that it clearly developed the skills of the pupils and delivered the best possible achievement in the time set. Is this not what we want every teacher to be able to deliver?

At the end of the season, when it was clear that both teams had come top of their league, the pupils were on top of the world and incredibly happy to be part of a team that had travelled such a successful journey.

The school was incredibly proud that the pupils had responded so well to such inspirational coaching and made such progress in what they did. Whether inside or outside the classroom, teachers should find opportunities in the curriculum or in the extra-curricular activities for pupils to be allowed, if not expected, to reach for the stars and make amazing progress in their skills.

Occasionally they might just get there.

STRATEGY 5.4: Making the learning explicit

This is a simple and effective tool for teachers to help make the learning and therefore the progress going on in the classroom, in any activity, explicit.

Continued on next page

Outcome

Clarity for the pupils and the teacher as to how well the pupils have understood what is being taught. It enables the teacher to see at a glance how effectively the teaching of the skills has been.

Use of the strategy: at the end of an activity or lesson

Whenever pupils are being taught a skill. Especially useful as a pre-test (start of the lesson)/post-test (end of the lesson) question and answer session.

A useful strategy for also developing: accuracy.

Resources

Red/green cards.

How it works

- At the end of an activity, the teacher asks the pupils to place at the front of the desk a red card (indicating the pupil's inability to understand/demonstrate the skill being learnt), both a red and a green card (indicating the pupil's partial understanding/ability to demonstrate the skill being learnt) or a green card (indicating the pupil's understanding/ability to demonstrate the skill being learnt).

- N.B. This can also be done in lessons without desks, such as PE, Music, Drama, etc., using thumbs down (indicating the pupil's inability to understand/demonstrate the skill being learnt), thumbs horizontal ((indicating the pupil's partial understanding/ability to demonstrate the skill being learnt) or thumbs up (indicating the pupil's understanding/ability to demonstrate the skill being learnt).

- This can be repeated at the end of the lesson to summarise the learning that has taken place.

How will the teacher ensure learning has taken place?

Through ensuring all pupils are clear about what is to be learnt and how pupils will know and recognise it is learnt (green card). If this is not the case, pupils use a red card.

How will progress be seen to be made?

Progress in this activity will be visible through pupils increasingly displaying green cards/thumbs up) as the teacher more effectively teaches the class.

STRATEGY 5.5: Pupil leaders

This lesson never fails to impress. Pupils who are more skilled and able at a subject are trained to be pupil leaders. In these lessons, they are expected to take a lead role and help the teachers teach the lesson and work with the other pupils in the class. This helps embed subject-specific knowledge and skills for the pupils as well as ensuring all the pupils in the lesson are supported.

Outcome

By the end of the lesson, the pupils are more skilled at understanding and demonstrating a skill in a subject than they were at the beginning of the lesson.

Use of the strategy: mid-way to the end of a lesson or topic

This strategy is useful when there are at least one or two pupils who are starting to demonstrate that they are particularly skilled at a topic or particularly skilled in the subject more generally.

A useful strategy for also developing: resilience and knowledge quickly.

Resources

Guidance sheets, badges and pupils who are talented in a topic or in a subject.

How it works

- Once it becomes clear a pupil has mastered a skill faster and more proficiently than others in the class, the teacher makes them pupil "Leaders" for that topic.

- The teacher then goes through the expectations and what to do in the role. This includes the teacher being able to successfully coach and train the pupil experts in what is needed.

- Pupils can then lead activities in lessons, for example, the starter or plenary, or be deployed during the lesson to help other pupils.

How will the teacher ensure learning has taken place?

Through noticing the quality of the work of the supported pupils and the pupil leaders improved significantly.

How will progress be seen to be made?

In the increased skill, knowledge and confidence of the pupil leaders in what they do as well as noticing others in the class able to demonstrate more complex work than would otherwise be the case.

STRATEGY 5.6: Scaffolding down

A common strategy that teachers use, especially at the start of a project, is to start simply and work up from there. This strategy turns this on its head, especially effective when working with more able groups or with groups that are two to three weeks into a topic.

Outcome

By the end of the lesson, more pupils will have achieved the lesson objective than would have otherwise been the case.

Use of the strategy: mid-way through to the end of a topic

This strategy is particularly useful when pupils are increasingly confident with the skills they are being taught and can therefore manage the higher expectations and more significant challenge this strategy provides.

A useful strategy for also developing: resilience and knowledge quickly.

Resources

PowerPoint and any required resources for the lesson.

How it works

- The aim, objectives and high expectations of the lesson are set so that the most able pupil is significantly challenged. It will therefore seem impossible for the pupils who are not as capable.

- The teacher explains that all pupils are expected to engage and explain the resilience needed and the skills development this lesson provides.

- During the lesson, the teacher then provides the scaffolding (steps/activities/explanations) to help the rest of the pupils rise quickly to the challenges set and successfully achieve the aim of the lesson.

How will the teacher ensure learning has taken place?

Through setting the very high expectations and ensuring the necessary scaffolding and support is in place so that all pupils can achieve the aims and objectives set.

How will progress be seen to be made?

Progress in this activity will be visible through the high expectations being met, with more pupils able to independently demonstrate by the end of the lesson the higher order skills than would otherwise have been the case.

STRATEGY 5.7: The model plenary

I have used this activity for years and when Ofsted saw me do it one year, they stole it!

Here it is for you. Because it is simple to use, the pupils quickly get the hang of it and it always makes an enjoyable end to the lesson.

Outcome

The outcome of the exercise is for the pupils to reflect on and be able to verbalise in a confident and convincing way the learning that has taken place for them during the lesson.

Use of the strategy: five minutes at the end of a lesson

This works well with a soft ball which the teacher can use to select the specific pupils to answer the question. As it uses neutral sentence stems, it can be used in a variety of situations.

A useful strategy for also developing: knowledge and accuracy.

Resources

PowerPoint slide/poster and a soft ball.

How it works

Presenting a set of sentence stems on the board, the teacher selects pupils, one at a time, to reflect on and verbalise the learning and progress they have achieved in the lesson.

These sentence stems can include:

Looking back over the lesson:

- What I have learnt is...., because....

- What I can now do is...., because....

- What I now know is...., because....

- What I found challenging was...., because...

- What I need to improve next lesson is...., because....

How will the teacher ensure learning has taken place?

Through ensuring every pupil can evaluate their learning and give confident, high-quality answers.

How will progress be seen to be made?

Through every pupil being able to answer the questions posed, thoroughly and thoughtfully.

STRATEGY 5.8: Displaying annotated work

This is one of the best ways to share best practice and help pupils see the skills and standard of skills needed to achieve the different grades. It is especially useful on corridors as the frequently passing pupils help promote and distribute the information more effectively than on a classroom display board.

Outcome

The outcome is for pupils to be able to understand and more accurately identify the skills and the standard of skills required for a specific grade/level in their own and others' work.

Use of the strategy: at the end of a lesson or topic

Being a display, this strategy can be used for a whole year or for a term, depending on the relevance of the skills in question to each subsequent topic.

A useful strategy for also developing: knowledge and accuracy.

Resources

A range of completed pupil work that has been marked and annotated. Display boards and display materials.

How it works

■ Pupil work that has achieved a variety of grades is displayed.

■ It also includes the marks it has achieved with annotated labels outlining the specific parts of the work which have achieved specific marks. In this way, it will be clear how the overall grade has been achieved.

■ Having a variety of work displayed will enable pupils to see the difference between the grades and the difference in quality/quantity of responses to achieve those grades.

How will the teacher ensure learning has taken place?

Through referencing the display in lessons and for homework, making an activity around the display and evaluating the displayed work and relating it to pupils' own work.

How will progress be seen to be made?

Pupils identify independently how their own work can improve and are more able to make those improvements happen, having seen it and thought through how those improvements can be made.

PROGRESS IN PRACTICE: lessons learnt in skills – extra-curricular activities

Extra-curricular activities enable skills learnt in the classroom to be practised and developed independently outside of the classroom. Any school that wants to create the positive conditions for those skills learnt in the classroom to grow and strengthen must have a healthy extra-curricular activities programme.

Extra-curricular activities complement and provide additionality to the curriculum

When I was the head of performing arts, I happened to walk past the bike sheds and noticed that there was a set of steel pans stacked up in them and rusting away nicely. If you don't know this, steel pans are very expensive, so to find a full set was a great find – in whatever condition. I went in at the weekend and de-rusted them and looked around for somebody who could tune them. When the steel pan tuner arrived (a niche but valuable job involving the most delicate of hammering), he introduced himself as the person who had originally brought the steel pans over from the Caribbean and would be very happy to tune them and hear them played at the school again. After a year, we invited him to our summer concert in the playground, where, much to his enjoyment, the steel pans sung beautifully again. The pupils, enjoying the experience so much, went on to study GCSE music, using them as their principle instrument and gained strong grades as a result.

Extra-curricular activities create and strengthen learning communities

A similar story occurred when the school was invited to perform in an outdoor festival, should the school have a samba band. Having no samba band but teaching samba as part of the curriculum in Year 9, it was relatively easy to form a band to perform at the outdoor festival. The chemistry that developed, and the musical skills that strengthened and progressed as a result, meant that the pupils en masse chose to study music as their option choice and similarly went on to gain good grades in their exams.

Extra-curricular activities uncover and develop talent

Once, at auditions for the annual show, a pupil didn't want to audition with the others, as they were so shy. So, he came along just before we packed up and asked if he could sing for us. As he sang, which was the voice of an angel, he was completely focused and in the song. At the end of the song, there was great applause not only from us, watching from the front, but also from the 50 pupils who had silently gathered behind him while he was singing. I will never forget his face, and the shock and surprise that he felt, when he turned around and saw so many people cheering.

Extra-curricular activities are needed in schools. To find and develop talent and weave a little magic.

Implications for leaders: demonstrating impact

For the leader monitoring progress in skills, there are several tools available.

Quantitative measures: data analysis

Analysis of the assessment data is the clearest method of demonstrating impact (EEF, 2019d).

Patterns in the data will emerge between individual pupils, small or large groups of pupils, showing themes and variations in their assessment outcomes. A question that would arise for leaders is why are those patterns taking place? This may indicate that the transference of understanding in terms of skills development may be an issue. Leaders should then look to the programmes of study, schemes of work and assessment programme to check for comprehensiveness, coherence and clarity in teaching skills. This should then be followed up with lesson observations to check that the programme of study or scheme of work is being followed consistently.

Quantitative measures: scheme of work/assessment tracker checks

The scheme of work and assessment trackers in books should show sequentially the skills to be learnt and the assessments to evaluate the learning process. The data on the tracking sheets should be up-to-date and show over time that the assessments have increased in difficulty.

Qualitative measures: book scrutinies

A great starting place to see progress in skills is in pupils' books. This can be through several methods:

Standard of work in pupils' books: Looking through the pupils' books, there should be a clear progress in the increasing level of difficulty of the work from the start of the book to the most current work.

More complex language: The language used related to the skills being learnt is increasingly more complex through the book. More keywords are more accurately used and indicate progress in understanding and expression of the skills being learnt.

More complex writing: The complexity of the writing with more compound and complex sentences, increased vocabulary and use of adjectives and adverbs, as pupils think more clearly and skilfully are indicators of progress in writing skills.

More technical feedback: The reflections of and feedback given to the pupils, through self-assessment, peer assessment or teacher assessment, and the responses to that feedback, are increasingly technical, showing a higher degree of understanding of the skills being understood and reached.

These initial findings can then be triangulated by looking in numerous pupils' books to see how well the development of the skills have been a focus of the teacher and a department or faculty.

Qualitative measures: observations

Observations of the lesson will also indicate whether skills are being explicitly taught by the teacher and learnt by the pupils during the lesson or not. During the lesson, the teacher should be teaching, and the pupil should be learning increasingly difficult work as both the lesson, and especially the year, progresses.

Qualitative measures: learning walks

Learning walks around a department or a school will identify patterns across several classes. Patterns may emerge which require praise and/or follow-up with a faculty or group of teachers in respect of teaching skills.

During a learning walk, key skills-related issues to check include ensuring that all classes are following the school's expectations as well as being on track with the department's scheme of work and programme of study.

Key questions

For teachers

1 How are you explicitly teaching specific skills to pupils?

2 How are you communicating the assessment criteria for the skills being developed and how are pupils to demonstrate those skills?

3 How are you ensuring in your lessons that you are explicitly incrementally challenging pupils and they clearly know what those challenges are?

4 How are you making best use of the activities and displays to communicate the trajectory of increasingly difficult skills the pupils need to master?

5 How regularly are you consciously transferring to the pupils the skills they need to learn and the ability to develop those skills without you?

For leaders and governors

1 How are leaders regularly checking schemes of work, programmes of study and assessment criteria and ensuring all the generic and subject-specific skills that need to be learnt are being learnt?

2 Are all leaders and teachers clear about the school's policy/expectations on both the generic skills (reading, writing, speaking, numeracy and listening) and the subject-specific skills they are teaching, and the pupils are learning? How do you know?

3 What is the quality of the books in relation to progress in skills being taught (writing, language difficulty/complexity, assessments taken and achieved) through the books?

4 What patterns emerge from the data and what does that tell you about how well pupils are increasingly skilled in their work?

5 When you are observing lessons, can you see progress being made in the pupils' skills?

6 How broad and balanced is your extra-curricular activities programme? What more can be done to ensure pupils can develop their skills further beyond the classroom?

For parents

1 What does the school recommend you can do as a parent to help improve your child's generic skills of reading, writing, speaking and listening with their homework?

2 What guidance does the school provide about the subject-specific skills being taught to your child?

3 What questions can you ask your child to help them have a clearer understanding of the challenges they are facing with their schoolwork, who to talk to and how to work through them?

4 What clubs are available at the school, or locally, to help develop the skills/ talents your child has in a particular area?

ENDNOTE

Progress in practice: lessons learnt in skills – Rachmaninov

What was the first record you ever bought?

At the age of 15, mine was Rachmaninov's Second Piano Concerto.

I know. My dad asked me the same question. "What?" In reassuring you (and him), this was very closely followed by Queen's Greatest Hits. At the time, my response to my dad was "Yes, but have you heard it? The first and third movements are just amazing!"

I don't know from where I picked up my love of classical music, but it was there. I listened to this piece so often (some might say obsessively), conducting it in the solitude of night, only me and a pair of headphones, carried away by the music and dreaming of conducting on the podium with pianist and orchestra in front and a rapturous crowd behind, like Harry Potter, weaving musical magic into the air.

Fast forward 16 years and I am discussing with a fellow Head of Music about having a joint Easter concert together, combining our two schools. Not doing things by halves, we agree to hire out St Alban's Abbey (and why not?). She agrees to conduct the joint schools' choir, I get the joint schools' orchestra.

When looking for music for the orchestra to play, imagine my excitement at finding in the local music library, a school's orchestral version of Rachmaninov's Second Piano Concerto. I take it. First port of call is a Sixth Former who is amazingly skilled at the piano. "Can you do it? Give it a go? Yes?" (he says yes). Bingo. Port of call number two, the orchestra. "Can you play it? Possible? Yes?" (they say yes). Bingo.

And there we are, our joint schools Easter Concert with choirs, bands, ensembles and soloists in St Alban's Abbey in front of us and an audience waiting to be enraptured behind us. And there was a 15-year-old boy on the podium, no longer conducting on his own in the dark, but, like Harry Potter, weaving musical magic into the air. And a dream came true.

This is why we teach. This is why we help pupils be as skilled as they can be in their work. To enable them to experience an amazing, wonderful world, of which they are a part and in which they have their place.

6 Progress in the lesson: knowledge

Progress in knowledge plain and simple:

Progress in knowledge is in the pupil being more knowledgeable, able to produce more detailed and more informed responses.

You may have the skills, but do you have the knowledge?

In this chapter we will cover:

- What we mean by knowledge
- Consciously teaching knowledge
- Enabling pupils to be more knowledgeable
- Modelling knowledge
- Teaching knowledge in practice: activities and strategies
- Implications for leaders on knowledge
- Questions to help further understand and improve knowledge

Introduction

The second measure of progress in the classroom to discuss is knowledge, e.g. to be able to write knowledgeably.

This chapter is about the pupil's ability to understand more about the subject they are learning and be able to demonstrate that knowledge. This could be through responses to questions in tests, but it could also be in response to tasks being set, or to questions posed by the teacher.

The focus of this chapter is to make clear progress in learning related to knowledge and the pupils' understanding of that knowledge. This is the incremental improvement in their understanding and their ability to demonstrate and make that understanding explicit. For example, in playing the piano, the pupil not only knows how to play a piano (skill), but what the different markings mean (louder, softer, faster, slower) and the composer's intent/history behind the piece, enabling the performance to also have more feeling and meaning, able to play the piano more knowledgeably.

The reason for this focus is that it requires a different teaching technique to the teaching of skills and therefore requires treating and examining separately. It will then be possible to bring this together with our understanding of progress in skills outlined in the previous chapter.

✓ In the classroom, when teaching knowledge, it is important that pupils understand why the teacher is asking them to understand something further (know more).

✓ It's important to teach pupils not just how to do something, but what the context is, the theory behind a skill and the uses it will have for them.

✓ Increasing their knowledge about their work is a significant key to helping pupils know how to be more successful in their work.

What we mean by progress in knowledge

MEASURE OF PROGRESS: THE AMOUNT OF KNOWLEDGE KNOWN

FROM THE TEACHER	FROM THE PUPIL
INCREASING AMOUNTS OF INFORMATION	AN INCREASE IN KNOWLEDGE
MORE COMPLEX INFORMATION	DEEPER KNOWLEDGE
CLEARER EXPLANATIONS	GREATER UNDERSTANDING
MORE DETAILED QUESTIONING	MORE DETAILED RESPONSES

This second measure of progress and a different measure to skill is the degree with which a pupil demonstrates their increased understanding and knowledge in a subject.

Knowledge or understanding has a set of different measures and criteria. To know. To understand. Something more is known. Something more is understood. Responses are more detailed; skills are more informed. Knowledge is a more intangible measure, less demonstrable, when compared to skills. Pupils either know something or they don't, they know more, or they don't. But this is not necessarily explicit until questions are asked.

This second measure, knowledge, therefore, requires careful questioning from the teacher to elicit how much knowledge a pupil has learnt.

Pupil work is increasingly longer, fuller. There are more detailed pupil responses to the teacher's questions over time. The success criteria therefore for this measure is in pupil responses being more detailed, more informative and more knowledgeable over time. This can be elucidated either from the quality of the verbal answers given to teachers' questions, or from the quality of the written work demonstrating the increasing understanding and knowledge that is written in pupils' books.

What the research says about the teaching and learning of knowledge

After skills, this is the most researched area in which teachers and pupils can demonstrate progress in learning.

In addition to what the research says about progress in general, as outlined in Chapter 3, there are a couple of points raised specifically about progress related to knowledge.

There is broad agreement that knowledge, alongside skills and accuracy, are intertwined and are the "warp and weft" of every lesson, in every school, every day (Dunford, 2016, p.66, Kirby, 2016, p.16).

The suggested method of teaching knowledge is that it needs to be both *challenging* and *coherent* (Anderson, 2001, Kirby, 2016, p.21), for example using a knowledge learning framework such as Bloom's taxonomy. There is also empirical evidence, known as dual coding, that by transmitting learning to both a non-verbal, e.g. visual input (imagery) at the same time as a verbal, e.g. aural input (teacher or pupil speaking), pupils will learn more effectively (Paivio, 1986, Clark, 1991, Mayer, 1998, Holcomb, 1999, Kirschner, 2002). The implications here are enormous; pupils will learn far more effectively watching a film (animated non-verbal imagery and verbal voiceover) compared to other more uniform techniques. As a result, the research suggests that teachers should use more dual coding wherever possible, to help put their respective learning points across.

Ofsted concur with this, finding that progress in maths improves when teachers use both language and practical aids (Ofsted, 2017). The research is also clear that due to the brain taking in reading and speaking *through the same input* makes learning *less* effective. Teachers therefore need to resist the temptation to speak while pupils are reading (Clark, 1991, Holcomb, 1999, Kirschner, 2002, Enser, 2019).

Bloom's taxonomy (Anderson, 2001) helps incrementally map cognitive skills such as applying or analysing knowledge while at the same time incrementally mapping knowledge. This has been one of the 20th century's most influential perspectives on learning. See Strategy 6.2 (p.86) for more on this.

Tests and quizzes are the best way to help pupils remember knowledge (Kirby, 2016, p.24). Other strategies to help remember knowledge effectively includes interleaving two topics (Richland, 2003, Rohrer, 2014), homework, drill, having the whole class or individuals recap knowledge, reading or receiving instruction in small bite-size segments (UKCES, 2014, Dyer, 2016, p.28).

> Further, using dual media programmes, such as Spark video, can be a more effective way of communicating knowledge and information between the teacher and their pupils and vice versa (Lane, 2019).

Consciously teaching knowledge: how knowledge is taught

In the lesson, knowledge is taught by providing opportunities for pupils to learn about a topic, helping them understand and become more knowledgeable about the theories, concepts, facts, keywords and key moments in history, or key people related to that topic.

It is then for the teacher to provide opportunities for pupils to express and demonstrate that understanding in front of others. For example, through the regular use of plenaries, question time, or through scaffolded questioning using aids or resources such as word walls or literacy mats.

> Teaching knowledge is the perfect vehicle for the teacher to inspire. It is where the teacher can truly be the star! This is their specialism. This is their area of expertise. If ever there was an area for the teacher to shine and motivate the pupils, it is in this area of specialist subject knowledge. Thus, it is in the teacher's passion for their subject, their indefatigable encouragement and infectious enthusiasm that will help the pupils not only *learn about* a subject but *enjoy learning* a subject.

The incremental improvements in understanding are in the pupils being more knowledgeable, being more engaged with the work as understanding and knowledge increase; able to give responses that are increasingly detailed and show an increasing understanding of the concepts, theories and facts.

It is also demonstrated through the increasingly knowledgeable answers given to questions, with answers that are increasingly complex and wide-ranging.

So, the measure of progress in understanding is in the quality of response of the pupils. More knowledge leads to more engagement, better quality responses, better understanding about the lessons being learned.

Activities and strategies that promote progress in knowledge

This section offers a range of strategies and activities that promote progress in knowledge. As with the previous activities and strategies related to skills, they can be used when the situation requires them. *It is for the teacher to use their professional judgement in deciding when the best time is to apply them.*

The strategies and activities are in a suggested succedent order. The strategies and activities at the start of this section being recommended for use at the start of a lesson or topic and the strategies and activities at the end of this section useful at the end of a lesson or topic.

Progress in knowledge requires much input at the start of a scheme of work as pupils need to know new concepts and terminology sooner rather than later. Managing this adeptly through effective drill and homework activities early on will get the pupils quickly through an important learning stage that can be reinforced and used well in subsequent lessons.

As with earlier activities and strategies, many of them may not be new to the reader. However, in recommending each strategy to help promote progress in a particular area and suggesting a timing when the strategy or activity is likely to be most effective, is new.

Again, for experienced teachers, this section provides several recommendations which can be used to refresh the memory of strategies and activities used in the past that can be brought back to the fore. The suggested activities will also provide confirmation of the good practice in your own choice of teaching strategies.

For less experienced teachers, I hope you find this section useful and full of easy-to-apply ideas that will help you and your classes see far more progress being made in a shorter duration of time with respect to pupil knowledge.

STRATEGY 6.1: The big question

A key, overarching question from which all other questions (and therefore teaching and learning) flow. Every theme in a topic flow from this. Having a single, plain and simple big question.

Outcome

This strategy provides a coherent learning framework to the topic in hand. By the end of the lesson, or the scheme of work, every pupil should be able to answer the big question coherently and effectively.

Continued on next page

Use of the strategy: at the start of a lesson or topic

Especially useful at the start of a topic or at the start of the lesson to set the scene and engage the pupils in the themes and questions that arise from the exploration of the new topic.

A useful strategy for also developing: independent learning.

Resources

PowerPoint or whiteboard and question.

How it works

■ The teacher has the big question displayed on the board asking the class to write down what answers and what further questions might arise as a result.

■ Thus, instead of a learning aim or outcomes, a big or fertile question at the very start of a scheme of work or lesson sets the scene or context and sets in motion a train of questions which all lead the pupils off in the direction of the new scheme of work. For example: How do cities change over time? Why are some countries less developed than others? Why do coastlines change?

■ Using a mind map or similar visual technique, the questions that need to be answered and the answers that need to be checked are mapped out.

How will the teacher ensure learning has taken place?

Through questioning and ensuring all the pupils are engaging with and responding to the question.

How will progress be seen to be made?

Pupils' answers to the big question will be far broader in scope, far more knowledgeable in breadth and far more detailed as a result of this strategy being used, than would otherwise be the case.

STRATEGY 6.2: Bloom's taxonomy of educational objectives

One of the most influential works of the twentieth century in education, Bloom's taxonomy spells out for pupils and teachers a hierarchy of knowledge and how to understand that knowledge.

Almost all lessons in some shape or form fit into this classic taxonomy.

Continued on next page

Outcome

At the end of the lesson/topic, the pupils will be able to understand, use and apply more difficult or complex words, more knowledgeably and accurately in response to the tasks and questions set.

Use of the strategy: at the start and throughout a topic

This strategy is useful whenever pupils need to understand the hierarchical stages in learning related to knowledge and the cognitive processes tied to these.

A useful strategy for also developing: accuracy, independent learning and resilience.

Resources

A copy of the taxonomy completed in relation to the topic being taught.

How it works

- The teacher creates twenty-four descriptors related to the topic being learnt that become increasingly more challenging against the knowledge dimension and more difficult against the cognitive process dimension.

- The pupil should be able to gauge their standard of work against this taxonomy and, as a result, able to plot the next level of work they need to complete, that is increasingly harder (more knowledgeable or more complex).

How will the teacher ensure learning has taken place?

Through creating a display or poster which can be used with pupils through question and response to help accurately identify demonstrated actions against the criteria outlined in the taxonomy. The teacher can also ensure learning has taken place through repetition of these activities and ensuring pupils peer assess and self-assess, checking their understanding is accurate as they do so.

How will progress be seen to be made?

Progress will be able to be seen through more pupils being able to understand, use more words and more complex words, more accurately in their work.

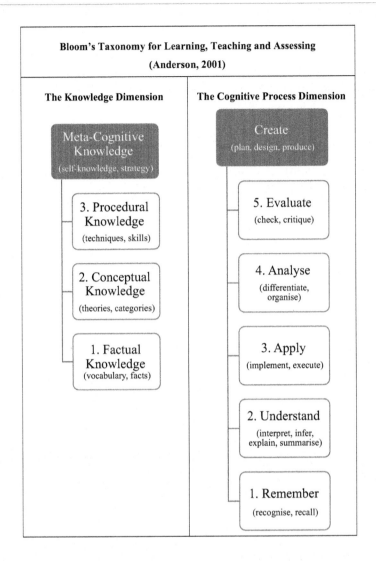

Bloom's Taxonomy for Learning, Teaching and Assessing
(Anderson, 2001)

The Knowledge Dimension

Meta-Cognitive Knowledge
(self-knowledge, strategy)

3. Procedural Knowledge
(techniques, skills)

2. Conceptual Knowledge
(theories, categories)

1. Factual Knowledge
(vocabulary, facts)

The Cognitive Process Dimension

Create
(plan, design, produce)

5. Evaluate
(check, critique)

4. Analyse
(differentiate, organise)

3. Apply
(implement, execute)

2. Understand
(interpret, infer, explain, summarise)

1. Remember
(recognise, recall)

STRATEGY 6.3: Word walls and literacy mats

Two of the most underused resources in a school to help transfer knowledge to pupils are word walls and literacy mats. Every lesson that needs a pupil to speak or write with more knowledge on a subject, the teacher should be insisting pupils use the word wall and/or literacy mats every time.

Outcome

At the end of the lesson/topic, the pupils will be able to understand, use and apply more words, more knowledgeably and accurately in response to the tasks and questions set.

Continued on next page

Use of the strategy: at the start and early stages of a topic

This strategy is useful whenever pupils are needed to speak/write in lessons.

For the less able, these act as props, supporting their learning until they feel more confident. For the more able, they act as a checklist of information they should know by heart.

A useful strategy for also developing: accuracy, independent learning and resilience.

Resources

Words ready for display and literacy mats for the topic being taught created and copied.

How it works

Word walls:

- A list of keywords for the topic being studied are placed on individual pieces of paper.

- The teacher orders the words coherently and displays 3–5 each week.

- The pupils find out about the words and are expected to be able to fully use them in their work by the end of the week.

Literacy mats:

- The keywords, key information, definitions, theories and concepts of a topic are logically structured and placed onto one sheet of A4 or A3.

- This sheet is then copied × the number of pupils in a class.

- The sheet is then used as a placemat for every lesson with pupils expected to refer to and use it regularly.

How will progress be seen to be made?

Progress will be able to be seen through more pupils
being able to understand and use more words, more
accurately in their work.

STRATEGY 6.4: Low stakes quizzes

This is a fabulous strategy because it gives pupils an opportunity to feel successful at the very start of a lesson. The pupils really like it because of its consistency. Having a low stakes quiz every week means that pupils get into a good routine as well as providing consistency to their learning.

Outcome

At the end of the quiz, it will be clear for the pupils and the teacher how well the pupils have understood and know what was taught during the previous lesson(s).

Use of the strategy: at the start of a lesson and throughout a topic

Used routinely every week at the start or end of the lesson, to recall prior learning in a non-judgmental way.

A useful strategy for also developing: accuracy.

Resources

Quiz

How it works

■ As a starter or as a plenary, the teacher sets a quiz for the pupils to take, explaining that the score could be low, but that is not an issue.

■ The point of the quiz is to simply help pupils realise how much they remember.

■ Pupils are not allowed to look in books as everything needs to be done from memory.

■ Teachers can also interleave previously learnt lessons to reinforce previous learning.

How will the teacher ensure learning has taken place?

Through setting and carrying out the quiz weekly and therefore setting the expectation that pupils need to study and work at remembering what has been learnt. Through repetition and explanation where necessary.

How will progress be seen to be made?

Progress in this activity will be visible through pupils' test scores being higher as the weeks progress.

STRATEGY 6.5: Leading roles

This activity helps pupils better understand how to work and play together constructively and positively. It can be applied to any group that is finding it difficult to self-regulate and is recommended because it enables pupils to more clearly understand the dynamics and importance of teamwork.

Outcome

Pupils will be able to demonstrate more effective teamwork, through increased knowledge as to what it means to be in a team. Pupils as a result can self-regulate with far greater success.

Use of the strategy: in the first few lessons of a topic

Over one lesson. This model is also useful to help improve pupil behaviour, helping pupils understand how to more effectively behave.

A useful strategy for also developing: teamwork skills, resilience and independent learning.

Resources

Role cards

How it works

- The pupils are put into groups of at least six and make up one or two rules which are to be enforced during the game or lesson.

- There are four roles which four pupils in each group take:
  - Referee (explains and enforces the rules)
  - Team Captain (the spokesman and communicator for the team)
  - Scorer (assesses and feeds back)
  - The Star Player (demonstrates and explains the skill / knowledge needed)

- Nobody else can speak during the game or lesson.

- The game or lesson begins until completed.

How will the teacher ensure learning has taken place?

Through ensuring that everyone understands and plays by the rules that are set. This teaches the pupils the different facets of being a good team player.

How will progress be seen to be made?

Pupils will understand more, be able to contribute more to their team's work and be able to independently self-regulate their behaviour more.

STRATEGY 6.6: Running dictation

This strategy is good for getting pupils actively engaged in their learning as well using their memory muscle and getting key information accurately inside their heads.

Outcome

At the end of the activity, pupils will have more accurate information and memorised the correct use and spelling of keywords and phrases.

Use of the strategy: at the start and throughout a topic

Useful during a topic as an activity to get the pupils to actively memorise key information as quickly and as accurately as possible.

A useful strategy for also developing: accuracy.

Resources

Statement banks displayed around the classroom.

How it works

- The teacher pre-prepares and displays around the classroom several posters which have key information on them.

- Pupils work in pairs or larger groups.

- As the teacher asks a question, one pupil from each group must go to the displayed posters and find the right one in answer to the question.

- This is then memorised and brought back to the team.

- The first team to get the answer right wins the point.

- The team with the most points wins the prize.

How will the teacher ensure learning has taken place?

Through ensuring the displayed answers stay on the wall, so that pupils must memorise the answers. Also, through checking the answers given by the pupils and confirming their accuracy.

How will progress be seen to be made?

Through pupils using increasingly accurate vocabulary and knowledge over time.

STRATEGY 6.7: Drill, spacing and interleaving – turning knowledge into memory

These strategies are good for getting pupils through the drier bits of learning in a fun way. They also help develop their memory muscles and getting more key information inside their heads.

Outcome

At the end of the activity, pupils will have more accurate information and memorised the correct use and spelling of keywords and phrases.

Use of the strategy: at the start, throughout a topic and throughout the year

Useful during a topic as an activity to get the pupils to actively memorise key information as quickly and as accurately as possible. As importantly, useful for going over previously learnt work and helping pupils remember what they already know!

A useful strategy for also developing: accuracy.

Resources

Keywords/statements/definitions.

How it works

- Chunking

Especially at the start of a topic, when pupils are short of facts and knowledge, the teacher teaches the lesson in small chunks to aid short-term memory retention (Kirschner et al., 2006), keeping information and activities short. (Kirschner, 2002; Paas et al., 2003).

- Drill and Spaced Learning

The teacher gets pupils to repeat knowledge at increasingly longer intervals, from immediate recollection (repetition helping to root information in the short-term memory) to weeks or months later (helping transfer the information to the long-term memory) (Rawson & Kintsch, 2005, Rohrer & Taylor, 2006, Ofsted, 2019a).

- Interleaving

Traditionally, most schools use blocking, where the learning and revision of knowledge happen in blocks (e.g. AAABBBCCC), with Topic A after it has been studied, never seen again until the exam.

Continued on next page

In interleaving, the teacher interleaves previously taught topics with the current topic being learnt. For example, in revision ahead of a test, Topics A, B and C are revised in an interleaved way (e.g. ABCABCABC). There is growing evidence that this can improve retention (Richland et al., 2005, Rohrer et al., 2014) and therefore improve assessment grades and progress.

● Retrieval

Retrieval involves recalling something learned in the past and bringing it back to mind. Retrieval practice strengthens memory and makes it easier to retrieve the information later (Barenberg Roeder & Dutke, 2018).

Retrieval practice needs to occur at a reasonable time after the topic has been initially taught and needs ideally to take the form of testing knowledge, either by the teacher or through pupil self-testing. It is important that feedback on the accuracy of the recall is provided either by the teacher or by the pupil checking the accuracy for themselves.

How will the teacher ensure learning has taken place?

Through ensuring the students memorise the key information effectively. Also, through checking the answers given by the pupils and confirming their accuracy.

How will progress be seen to be made?

Through pupils using increasingly accurate vocabulary and knowledge over time.

STRATEGY 6.8: Flash cards

This strategy is a classic. It is simple. It is easy. It can be used with numerous classes year in year out. Being visual and with minimal words, it is accessible for all pupils.

Outcome

At the end of the activity, the pupils and the teacher will be more aware of the key symbols, words, concepts and theories, as well as being aware of how well the pupils know them.

Use of the strategy: throughout a topic

This strategy is great at the start of a topic to introduce key symbols, words and concepts; during a topic to reinforce them; or towards the end of a topic or scheme in revising and reinforcing the key symbols, words, concepts and theories learnt over the course of the topic.

A useful strategy for also developing: accuracy.

Continued on next page

Resources

Flash cards

How it works

■ The teacher creates a set of A5 or A6 cards with keywords, symbols, theories and concepts on them.

■ They show them one at a time for 10 seconds, while pupils write the answer down as to what they meant.

■ At the end of the activity, the class mark the answers.

■ The minimum required score would be determined by how early or late in the topic the quiz was being taken.

How will the teacher ensure learning has taken place?

Through ensuring clear explanations and reinforcement of learning were given for each of the cards in previous lessons and for homework.

How will progress be seen to be made?

Through the pupils knowing more and as a result, achieving increasingly higher test scores over time. Also, through increasingly accurate and more detailed answers to questions posed by the teacher.

STRATEGY 6.9: Stretch and super-stretch

These are two cards that every teacher should always have up their sleeve, or more precisely, always on the board. This strategy ensures every pupil in the class has work (and learning) to do.

Outcome

The outcome of this strategy is in ensuring every pupil has work, and therefore learning to do. Once the pupils have completed the main activity, they have additional, related, work to do. As a result, these provide the "stretch" or "super-stretch" activities.

Use of the strategy: throughout a topic, at the end of an activity, in any lesson.

Useful for all classes and additionally useful in helping the teacher either chart the next phase of learning earlier or cover additional educational ground in the current topic.

Continued on next page

A useful strategy for also developing: skills, knowledge, resilience and independent learning.

Resources

Additional questions.

How it works

■ At the end of the instructions to the starter or main tasks of the lesson, the teacher includes a "stretch" and/or "super-stretch" activity.

■ This provides a challenging extension to the main activities by giving the pupils more challenging tasks or harder texts.

■ The high expectation for the class is that everyone should complete the main tasks set and move onto at least the stretch activity in the allocated time.

For example, adding more detail to an answer already given; using the upper end of Bloom's taxonomy and asking pupils to explain their answers/reasoning; asking pupils to pose an alternative and opposite point of view to the one already made.

How will the teacher ensure learning has taken place?

Through having timed activities, routinely setting challenging stretch and super-stretch activities and ensuring all pupils complete the main activities and complete at least the stretch activity.

How will progress be seen to be made?

More work and more difficult work completed in pupils' books, Also, through all pupils being on task for the whole lesson and all pupils completing at least the stretch activity.

STRATEGY 6.10: Strategy!

Blending strategy games, such as Chess and Risk, with key battles in history, this activity puts pupils at the centre of the decision-making for a battle and helps them more readily understand the decisions and mistakes that the great and the not-so-great leaders in history made. This strategy can be adapted for any subject where strategy and decision-making are central to an activity.

Continued on next page

Outcome

Pupils will be able to more fully understand battle strategies and the concepts and vocabulary that underpin them.

Use of the strategy: later in as topic

This activity is useful at the start of a topic, encouraging pupils to engage in a new or relatively little-known topic in a fun way. It is also useful later in a unit, to enable consolidation of knowledge and facilitate student's understanding of consequence and significance.

Resources

Battle cards and rules of the game.

How it works

- Pupils are dealt a set of cards.

- The aim of the game is to do battle with several opponent teams but to play your hand so that you win the game.

- Pupils decide which cards to play and against whom.

- Pupils then win or lose depending how the opposite team respond.

- Each team takes it in turns to decide what to do and how to play their cards until there is a winner.

- The winning strategy can then be compared to the actual strategy employed by the leaders in the real battles in history.

How will the teacher ensure learning has taken place?

Through ensuring notes are taken as to decisions made with reasons why, and a follow-up discussion to explore and examine these in more detail.

How will progress be seen to be made?

Progress in teamwork. Pupils making more informed decisions and able to explain in a more informed and detailed way, the decisions they have made.

STRATEGY 6.11: Let the homework take the strain

When devising programmes of study or schemes of work, this strategy allows practical subjects especially, to use homework as the main method by which additional knowledge and theory can be learnt and reinforced, freeing up time in lessons to be used for practical, hands-on learning.

Outcome

Increased time in lessons to concentrate on practical work, through increased use of independent study time (homework) to cover theory and additional knowledge. Pupils are more knowledgeable and have a deeper understanding of the work as a result.

Use of the Strategy: throughout a topic, at the start and end of a lesson

Whenever theory or more knowledge is needed to be covered and there is little time in lessons available.

A useful strategy for also developing: independent learning.

Resources

Homework activities.

How it works

- The teacher purposely sets homework that adds more to pupils' knowledge (e.g. the historic or cultural context of a topic) or reinforces the theories that have been learnt that lesson.

- Homework activities could also include being asked at the end of the lesson to do a presentation for homework, to show what they have learnt, so the additional knowledge is easily identified and encapsulated.

How will the teacher ensure learning has taken place?

Through having pupils present their homework to the teacher or the class, referring to the homework set at the start of the lesson (taking the register and checking homework), or explicitly referring to it in class through the set activities.

How will progress be seen to be made?

Having expectations that a demanding homework is routinely set and being clear that the quality of the work is more important than the quantity of the work. Through the increased knowledge and more detailed responses of the pupils in the (home) work being completed.

STRATEGY 6.12: Pre-/post-test quizzes

This is a simple tool for teachers to help make the learning of knowledge in the classroom explicit. A tried and tested method that isn't used nearly as much as it could be – the same (or similar) quiz at the start and end of the lesson.

Outcome

At the end of the lesson, it will be clear for the pupils and the teacher how well the pupils have understood and know what was taught during the lesson. This will enable the teacher to quickly assess whether the class are ready to move on, or whether more time needs to be spent clarifying, reinforcing or approaching the lesson being taught from a different angle. This strategy makes the effectiveness of the teaching of the concepts and knowledge clearer.

Use of the Strategy: at the start and end of a lesson

Whenever pupils are being taught theories, concepts or previously unknown knowledge. Especially useful as a quantitative, numeric measure of how well pupils have learnt something.

A useful strategy for also developing: accuracy and independent learning.

Resources

Quiz

How it works

- At the start of the lesson, the teacher sets a quiz on the information being learnt that lesson for the pupils to take, explaining that the score could be low, but that is not an issue.

- The same (or a similar) quiz is then repeated at the end of the lesson or activity.

- The difference in scores is taken in.

- The higher the initial and latter score, or the higher latter score, the better.

How will the teacher ensure learning has taken place?

By thoroughly ensuring all pupils are clear about what is being taught and learnt in the lesson and how pupils will know and recognise it is learnt.

How will progress be seen to be made?

Progress in this activity will be visible through pupils' test scores at the end of the lesson being higher than at the start.

PROGRESS IN PRACTICE: Lessons learnt in knowledge – Adam's story

All great teachers do what Adam did. Have a knack for making the complex simple. Have a knack for making the implicit explicit, so that learning and progress are easily seen and celebrated in the classroom.

A science experiment, or rather practical illustration of a process that Adam did to everybody's pleasure and enjoyment was his scientific teaching of rocks and rock composition. He had an ingenious way of demonstrating this with the pupils; the different ways you can use sweets to illustrate the different rocks and how they are formed. Let me explain.

For sedimentary rocks he got the pupils to lower several chewy sweets into a jar and see, with the application of a little pressure, the different layers of "rock" forming, and with a little more pressure, create a solid mass of "sedimentary" rock.

A second activity, heating and melting the chewy sweets in a crucible, it was possible to demonstrate how igneous rocks are formed, with the solid mass that the melting sweets produced. This illustrated perfectly the different method by which the two different types of rocks are formed and thus explain the difference in their qualities; something which the teacher would, through questioning and referring to the similarities and differences between the two rock formation processes would produce.

With a blend of the two rock formation processes, he was able to illustrate how metamorphic rocks were created, so all pupils were able to understand and explain the effect of heat and pressure on material and the change in the qualities as a result. By demonstrating and allowing pupils to interact with the physicality of a concept or theory, pupils were actively engaged with the understanding behind the physics, with more questions being raised and needing to be answered.

This was the perfect hook or catalyst for engaging pupils and enabled them to both respond knowledgeably to the questioning by the teacher, as well as provoking more questions by the pupils. The teacher was able to provide more accurate information and ensure that pupils' understanding, and knowledge was more accurate and more detailed then it was at the start of the lesson.

The lesson could have been delivered in a straightforward way by the teacher, possibly using videos to illustrate the point. However, this would not necessarily have had the imaginary and inventive impact to help secure the information in the pupils' memory.

There are multiple methods of choosing a thought-provoking, simple and effective activity that will do the work of three or four lessons. Every lesson is an opportunity to demonstrate theory or concepts in real life, enabling the teacher and the pupil to express their understanding together and take that understanding to another level.

It also enables pupils to visualise technical language more effectively, engaging more effectively with plenaries, questioning and literacy mats. Pupil

Continued on next page

response and pupil engagement is far more evident by the end of the lesson than at the start of the lesson.

What was so special with this style of lesson? The pupils were more able to understand and therefore more able to connect previous learning and bring it into this sphere of learning. In addition, they could add names or labels to previously learnt knowledge and concepts, be more accurate or have an opportunity to take the language to a more complex or demanding level.

The pupils all felt good about the fact that they were doing something that seemed to be so simple and yet all of them felt the lesson worked well because it was simple, clear and effective in engaging pupils and helping them understand something that may otherwise have been confusing, or dull, or both.

Progress in knowledge is about using thought provoking activities that will spark interest and engage learners in learning. It is not just reading from a book about a topic and the teacher teaching about a topic. One of the largest influences on pupil learning is the teachers' expertise in their subject.

Just like Adam, what better platform for a teacher to enthuse and inspire their pupils than through being passionate, knowledgeable and enthusiastic about the subject they love?

Implications for leaders: demonstrating impact

For the leader monitoring progress in knowledge and pupil understanding, there are several tools available.

Quantitative measures: data analysis

Analysis of the assessment data is the clearest method of demonstrating impact (EEF, 2019c).

Patterns in the data will emerge between individual pupils, small or large groups of pupils showing themes and variations in their assessment outcomes. A question that would arise for leaders is why are those patterns taking place? This may indicate that the transference of understanding in terms of knowledge development, may be an issue. Leaders should then look to the programmes of study, schemes of work and assessment programme to check for comprehensiveness, coherence and clarity in teaching knowledge. This should then be followed up with lesson observations to check that the programme of study or scheme of work is being followed consistently.

Qualitative measures: scheme of work/assessment trackers in books

The scheme of work and assessment trackers in books should outline the knowledge to be learnt. It should be clear that each activity or topic subsequently presents increasingly complex theories, concepts and knowledge.

Qualitative measures: book looks

A great starting place to see progress in knowledge is in pupils' books.

Quality of work in pupils' books: Looking through the pupils' books there should be clear progress in the increasing amount of detail in the work from the start of the book to the most current work.

More complex language: The language and breadth of language used is increasingly diverse and more complex through the book. More complex keywords are used more accurately and indicate progress in understanding and expression.

More complex writing: The complexity of writing with more compound and complex sentences, increased use of adjectives and adverbs, as pupils think more knowledgeably and skilfully, are indicators of progress in writing with greater understanding.

More detailed feedback: The feedback given to the pupils, through self-assessment, peer assessment or teacher assessment, and the responses to that feedback, is increasingly detailed, showing a higher degree of knowledge being understood and applied.

Book scrutiny

These initial findings can then be triangulated by looking in a number of pupils' books to see how well the development of the pupils' knowledge has been a focus of the teacher.

Progress in writing

Looking through the scheme of work and triangulating it with the work in pupils' books over time, identifying how the writing is (or isn't!) more knowledgeable over time through seeing increasingly detailed writing and complexity of language being developed.

Qualitative measures: observations

Observations of the lesson will also be able to indicate whether theories, concepts and knowledge are being explicitly taught by the teacher and learnt by the pupils during the lesson or not. During the lesson, the teacher should be teaching, and the pupil should be learning increasingly difficult theories, concepts and knowledge as both the lesson and especially the year progresses. This should correspond with the equivalent place in the scheme of work or programme of study.

Qualitative measures: learning walks

Learning walks around a department or a school will identify patterns across several classes. Patterns may emerge that require praise and/or follow-up with a particular faculty or group of teachers.

During a learning walk, key knowledge-related issues for leaders to ensure are happening, include ensuring all classes are following the school's expectations, as well as being on track with the department's scheme of work and programme of study.

Key questions

For teachers

1 What opportunities are you creating in your lessons to enthuse, inspire and motivate the pupils with your subject knowledge?

2 How are you communicating the assessment criteria for the knowledge the pupils need to know and how pupils are to demonstrate that knowledge?

3 How are you making best use of the activities, displays and presentations to communicate the trajectory of increasing knowledge the pupils need to understand and know?

For leaders and governors

1 How are leaders checking schemes of work and programmes of study and ensuring all the generic and subject specific knowledge that needs to be learnt is being learnt?

2 Are all leaders and teachers clear about both the generic and subject specific knowledge they are teaching, and the pupils are learning?

3 Do leaders and staff understand how to teach and enable pupils to be increasingly knowledgeable in their subject areas? Are the assessment criteria in place and clearly understood?

4 What does the monitoring and tracking of pupil books tell you about how well pupils know and understand their work and are able to demonstrate progress in their responses?

5 What is the quality of the books in relation to knowledge (writing, language difficulty / complexity) developing through the books?

6 What patterns emerge from the data and what does that tell you about how well pupils are increasingly knowledgeable in their work?

7 When you are observing lessons, how can you see progress being made in the pupils' knowledge?

8 When you are carrying out a learning walk of the school or a department, what evidence is there of pupils working with increasing knowledge/understanding in what they do?

For parents

1 What does the school recommend you can do as a parent to help improve your child's general knowledge?

2 What guidance does the school provide about the subject-specific knowledge being taught to your child?

3 What questions can you ask your child to help them have a clearer understanding of their learning?

ENDNOTE

Progress in practice: lessons learnt in knowledge – Aykut and Conrad's story

When I was a music teacher in a challenging inner London school, one exam class that did memorably well was a group of pupils who were particularly varied in their musical tastes. One Spring day at break in the music room, there was a very unusual conversation I witnessed between two pupils at the piano which went something like this:

Conrad: "So, I've been learning this new piece of music by Mozart and it goes like this (he plays). I think it's great because when he was wanting to demonstrate a light feel, he did this (he plays). Can't get over that (he plays again). I think that's brilliant".

Aykut: "Well that's alright. But Beethoven did something better when he played this" (Aykut plays).

Conrad: "Hmmm, you've got a point there. Though that Mozart was writing a bit earlier than Beethoven, so he can probably claim a bit more credit. I think Mozart really nailed it in this piece" (he plays again).

Aykut: "Still think Beethoven nailed it more – Mozart's just a much simpler version of him" (he plays again).

You get the picture. What I was witnessing were two pupils in a challenging London school debating the merits of Beethoven's versus Mozart's piano writing, a discussion I wasn't expecting in a million years. Equally, I don't ever recall explicitly teaching them this. However, I'm sure it was included in some form of homework that added to the more technical work we were doing in lessons. Homework that required research, learning about the cultural background and history of the people we were studying.

For pupils who are particularly talented in an area within the school curriculum, it is so important that the teachers who are the champions for those areas, make sure that every opportunity is taken to nurture and develop talented pupils and feed their knowledge and understanding of the new world in which they find themselves, with like-minded people.

This will help orientate them and become more confident as a result.

7 Progress in the lesson: accuracy

Progress in accuracy plain and simple:

Progress in accuracy is in being able to see increases in the pupil being more right in what they do and less wrong.

You may have the skills and the knowledge, but are they accurate?

In this chapter we will cover:

- What we mean by accuracy
- Consciously teaching accuracy
- Enabling pupils to be more accurate
- Modelling accuracy
- Teaching accuracy in practice: activities and strategies
- Implications for leaders on accuracy
- Questions to help further understand and improve accuracy

Introduction

The third progress measure in the classroom to discuss is accuracy, for example to be able to write knowledgeably and accurately.

There is a well-known comedy sketch by the comedians Morecambe and Wise with the conductor Andre Previn, when, after a wonderfully grand opening to the Greig Piano Concerto by the London Symphony Orchestra, Eric Morecambe plays the solo part on the grand piano with a very simplified version of it. When challenged by the conductor that he was playing all the wrong notes, Eric Morecambe responds with "I'm playing all the right notes. But not necessarily in the right order".

This encapsulates beautifully the essence of progress in accuracy leading to progress in learning. Learning to be accurate is different from how we learn an increasingly difficult skill or increasingly complex knowledge. There is a confidence about it, almost an arrogance, for a pupil to say, "I know I'm right". This chapter explores how teachers can support pupils to be more accurate and the ability to show that understanding when demonstrating their skills and knowledge.

> The focus of this chapter is to make clear the progress in learning related to accuracy. It is the incremental improvements in the accuracy of a pupil's written or spoken language, understanding or action. Understanding how to be more right or less wrong; demonstrating work that can be redrafted, corrected and having less mistakes.

The reason for this focus is that accuracy is almost always taught alongside skills or knowledge and, as a result, rarely taught with the emphasis it deserves. Furthermore, accuracy in language (more qualitative, contextual and open to interpretation) is different to accuracy in numbers, science, music or sport (more quantitative, i.e. accurate or inaccurate, right or wrong).

To go back to Eric Morecambe and Andre Previn for a moment. Both thought they were playing the music accurately. When playing the piano, you hit the keys with your fingers and notes are played. However, it may not necessarily be accurate in terms of what the composer intended.

In the classroom, when teaching a skill, it is vitally important that pupils understand why the teacher is asking them to do something a certain way (the right way) rather than a different way (the wrong way). It's vitally important to teach pupils not just *how* to do something, but also *why* that way is the right way in how to do something correctly or accurately.

What we mean by progress in accuracy

MEASURE OF PROGRESS: THE ACCURACY OF A RESPONSE

FROM THE TEACHER	FROM THE PUPIL
INCREASING NUMBER OF PROBLEMS	INCREASING NUMBER OF ACCURATE RESPONSES
INCREASING DIFFICULTY OF PROBLEMS	INCREASING LEVELS OF ACCURACY
SUCCESS CRITERIA TO SOLVING A PROBLEM	INCREASED UNDERSTANDING OF SOLUTIONS
CLEARER EXPLANATIONS OF ACCURACY	GREATER UNDERSTANDING OF ACCURACY
MORE VARIED EXAMPLES OF PROBLEMS	INCREASED UNDERSTANDING OF ACCURACY

This third measure of progress and a different measure to skill and knowledge is the degree of accuracy with which a pupil demonstrates a skill or their understanding. This has a set of different measures and criteria in the sense that a skill requires guidance from the teacher as to what to do to demonstrate that skill. It is an active, demonstrable measure. Something is harder, more complex. Similarly, knowledge is a more intangible measure, less demonstrable. Pupils either know something or they don't. This third measure, accuracy, is very different in that it fine-tunes the active and demonstrable with also being correct or incorrect. It is an *additional measure* to skill and knowledge. A skill is demonstrated accurately or inaccurately. Our understanding can be more or less accurate.

> This requires a teacher to share the success criteria with the pupils as to what defines something as accurate or inaccurate, more correct or less correct. This therefore requires a different teaching technique. A technique which is about teaching accuracy and how something can be right or wrong, better or worse, rather than easier or harder, known or unknown.

What the research says about the teaching and learning of accuracy

In addition to what the research says about progress in general, as outlined in Chapter 3, there are a couple of points raised specifically about progress related to accuracy.

There is broad agreement that accuracy, alongside skills and knowledge, are intertwined and are the "warp and weft" of every lesson, in every school, every day (Dunford, 2016, p.66, Kirby, 2016, p.16), but with unguided independent learning running the risk of increased inaccuracy in learning and homework (Kirschner, 2006).

> In researching accuracy in the literature, very few (if any) writers or researchers explicitly reference accuracy, assumedly incorporating the teaching of accuracy into the teaching of skills and knowledge.

If you don't believe me, no less of an august body as Ofsted, in their latest framework and research documents reference accuracy, and the inspection of accuracy in the classroom, less than a handful of times.

According to the Office for Standards in Education's (Ofsted's) latest inspection framework and research (Ofsted, 2019b), the word accurate is stated only three times in relation to teaching in its inspection framework and research. One could be forgiven for thinking that the government and other agencies are not interested in ensuring that in a world of unregulated internet information, when such information is used in schools to teach the pupils, is accurate. Or perhaps in concentrating on the development of skills (mentioned 48 times) and knowledge (mentioned 89 times), they are *assuming* pupils will also be taught how to be accurate and that it doesn't need to be emphasized in their inspection framework.

Likewise, a brief search of the research appears to produce little that helps explore and describe teaching accuracy. Thus, with little to be said further in respect of accuracy in research, we turn to the teaching of accuracy; how teachers can teach pupils to be accurate and know they are being accurate.

Consciously teaching accuracy: how accuracy is taught

It is important to be clear about how we are defining accuracy in the classroom. By being accurate, we are "observing a condition or quality of something being true, correct, or exact; freedom from error or defect; precision or exactness; correctness". If something is inaccurate, there is error.

> How are pupils to *know* that they have made an error? How do they *recognise* this in their work?

Similarly, accuracy is close to being right, "conforming with fact, reason, truth or some standard or principle", as opposed to being wrong, where something deviates from the truth or fact. How do we effectively teach this and more importantly, how do pupils learn this?

There are several ways that teachers can explicitly teach accuracy which are discussed in more detail below.

Comparing the accurate with the inaccurate: helping pupils know the difference.

Teachers can help pupils to know the difference between right and wrong, between the accurate and the inaccurate by putting both the right and the wrong answer together side by side. This enables the pupil to see, compare, discuss and understand more clearly *why* something is right and *why* something is wrong.

For example, which of these is accurate? Which is the correct phrase according to Shakespeare's Hamlet?

To be or not to be that is the question

To be, or not to be, that is the question:

To be? Or not to be? That is the question.

Two of these are accurate. One of these is correct.

How do we know we are accurate? Because we've been taught the rules of punctuation. But how do we know what we do is accurate? Do we not need sometimes to be explicit about those rules with pupils and ensure they are accurate in their application?

How do we know we chose the correct quote from Hamlet? After all, two of the statements are accurate.

Because we learnt what he said, can recall it accurately, identify it correctly and know which is right.

> Therefore, comparing the accurate with the inaccurate helps clarify the rule and reinforces both the rule and what things look like if the rule is not followed. Teaching accuracy in this way requires the teacher to be able to explain clearly and explicitly what it is to be accurate *and* what it is to be inaccurate, *modelling both* for pupils. This enables pupils to *know the difference* between *both* right and wrong, the accurate and inaccurate (Illeris, 2007, p.175).

Referring to success criteria: helping pupils know the rules

Making explicit to the pupils the success criteria by which something is accurate, for example, displayed on a notice board, is important in helping them know whether what they are doing is right or not.

This is not necessarily the same as being explicit about the assessment criteria, which is about identifying and assessing their progress in skills and understanding.

> Success criteria specifies the rules – the definition of what is right and wrong. Assessment criteria specifies the standards – the definition of progression in skills and knowledge.

For example, watching a football match on TV with the off-side rules displayed next to the screen – it will be far easier for the pupils to see, recognise and understand when the off-side rule applies and whether a referee calls it right or wrong because the pupil can see the rules alongside the play.

Using dictionaries, literacy mats and word walls: getting vocabulary right first time

As pupils grow and develop in their learning and understanding, their language also must grow and develop. Helping pupils accurately understand the meaning of words is one of the joys of teaching and shouldn't stop as the pupils get older. The expectation is that a pupil's vocabulary should grow with them. As a result, the ability to use a word wall, literacy mat, dictionary and thesaurus is a must in a classroom if we want pupils to develop a rich and accurate understanding of the language that surrounds them.

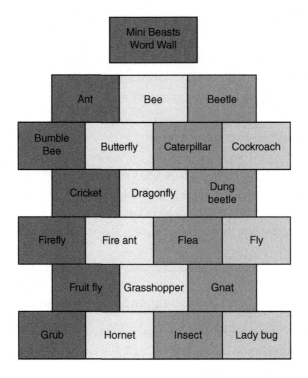

Figure 7.1 A Word Wall

Using word walls, literacy mats or dictionaries in a lesson ensures that pupils use keywords accurately and correctly first time. It provides them with the environment and opportunity in a lesson to explore and learn correctly how to use these words accurately from the very beginning.

Without them, and without using them accurately, we are setting in motion a future world of misunderstanding, misspelling and inaccuracy. This is before some pupils have even started. This doesn't need to be the case.

Is a pupil being inaccurate in what they do down to the pupil or the teacher? Neither or both? Put another way, if every teacher taught and every pupil learnt how to be accurate in everything they do, what would be the impact on the student's progress, on their results?

As a lesson, a scheme of work and a programme of study evolve, so the pupil's need to understand what is accurate and inaccurate increases. Teaching accuracy explicitly and thoroughly is the key. This enables pupils to ensure their work is increasingly coherent, re-drafted more accurately and show more correct, more accurate work as time progresses.

Communicating complex concepts: getting the right words in the right order!

Especially when teaching complex theories and concepts, a literacy mat or word wall will have all the right words, but laying it out alphabetically, as in the example in Figure 7.1, would not be the right order if teaching it phonetically (English) or mini beasts that fly and minibeasts that don't fly (Science). This alphabetical order would therefore need to be re-ordered more accurately if we are teaching keywords connected to a specific concept.

As such, when teaching complex concepts and theories, it is important for the teacher to be crystal clear, not only with the choice of words and what they mean, but also the order of the words in which they are placed within the process. Communicating the right words in the right order will ensure that the accuracy of both the pupil knowing *what the word means*, but also the accuracy of knowing what the word means *in the context of other words*, significantly helps pupils understand what they have been taught. Having *clear words* and a *clear order* is key. Plain and simple.

Displaying success criteria, laying out complex theories and concepts in a logical and clear way, comparing right and wrong answers, using dictionaries, word walls and literacy mats, all help to make accuracy explicit and develop more accurate understanding, reading and writing skills.

As a result, these will help the pupil make visible, tangible progress, unlike Eric Morecambe, to metaphorically play all the right notes *and* in the right order.

Activities and strategies that promote progress in accuracy

This section offers a range of strategies and activities that promote progress in accuracy. As with the previous activities and strategies related to skills and knowledge, they should be used when the situation requires them. *It is for the teacher to use their professional judgement in deciding when the best time is to apply them.*

The strategies and activities are ordered in a suggested succedent order based on the most effective place for it in the lesson/how easily it can be set up. The strategies and activities at the start being recommended for use at the start of a lesson or topic and the strategies and activities at the end useful at the end of a lesson or topic.

Progress in accuracy requires much input at the start of a scheme of work as pupils need to know the difference and how to tell the difference between the accurate and inaccurate, the right (way) and the wrong (way) sooner rather than later. Managing this adeptly through effective routines early on will get the pupils quickly through an important learning stage that can be reinforced and used well in subsequent lessons.

As with earlier activities and strategies, many of them may not be new to the reader. However, the value of each strategy lies in promoting progress in a particular area and suggesting a timing when the strategy or activity is likely to be most effective.

Again, for experienced teachers, this section provides several recommendations which you can use to refresh your memory of strategies and activities that you used in the past and maybe need to bring back again to the fore. The strategies and activities will also provide confirmation that in already doing these strategies and activities with your classes confirms the good practice in your own choice of teaching strategies.

For less experienced teachers, I hope you find this section useful and full of easy-to-apply ideas that will help you and your classes experience far more progress being made in a shorter duration of time with respect to accuracy.

STRATEGY 7.1: What – spot – got the mistake?

The beauty of these activities is in their simplicity. Two statements, sums or images, one accurate and one inaccurate, with a simple question – what's the difference? Guaranteed swift progress (Clark, 1991) and gets the pupils engaged quickly and any lesson off to a flying start.

Outcome

At the end of these activities, pupils will be able to see, discuss and understand the difference between accurate and inaccurate work. The activities make the required levels of accuracy explicit.

Timing of the activities

10–15 minutes each – perfect as a starter activity or a plenary.

Resources

Three pairs of accurate/inaccurate statements/images/sums, PowerPoint or Whiteboard and pens.

Continued on next page

How it works

What's the Mistake?	Spot the Mistake	Got the Mistake
Two statements, images, sums are placed side by side on the board, one is accurate, and one is inaccurate, with the question: What's the difference?	During the lesson, the teacher deliberately inserts information or a technique that is inaccurate.	During the lesson, using peer marking or self-assessment, the pupil searches for information or a technique that is accurate or inaccurate in another pupil's work.
Teacher then leads a discussion as to why one is accurate and why one is inaccurate. An opportunity is given to ask questions and consolidate learning.	At the start of the lesson, the teacher explains that through the lesson there will be X number of inaccurate statements/pieces of information to spot.	At the start of the lesson, the teacher explains that through the lesson there may be several inaccurate statements/pieces of information to spot as well as a certain amount of accurate statements/skills to spot. For both, the pupil needs to feedback to the other pupil on the specific aspects which were accurate/inaccurate.
A further pair of statements, images, sums are placed side by side on the board, one is accurate, and one is inaccurate, with the question: What's the difference?	So, as many pupils as possible participate, each pupil can only identify and correct one mistake at a time.	
This time the teacher only asks questions to draw out from the pupils why one is accurate and why one is inaccurate. An opportunity is given to further ask questions and consolidate learning.	After the first three or four, the teacher either confirms that the pupils have accurately spotted and corrected the mistakes in the lesson and to continue doing so, or that they had failed to spot them and need to revise what makes something (in)accurate.	So as many pupils as possible participate, the teacher changes the peer assessment pairings, so each pupil receives feedback from more than one student.
A final pair of statements, images, sums are placed side by side on the board, one is accurate, and one is inaccurate, with the question: What's the difference?	The teacher then continues through the lesson, with pupils identifying and correcting the deliberate mistakes.	After the first three or four, the teacher either confirms that the pupils have spotted accuracies and accurately corrected the mistakes in the lesson and to continue doing so, or that they had failed to spot them and need to revise what makes something (in)accurate.
This final time the teacher cannot speak, and the pupils lead the discussion and then write down why one is accurate and why one is inaccurate.		The teacher then continues through the lesson, with pupils identifying accuracies and correcting their own mistakes.

Continued on next page

How will the teacher ensure learning has taken place?

Through ensuring pupils are given an increasing number of opportunities to identify inaccuracies and provide the correct answers.

How will progress be seen to be made?

Progress in these activities will be visible through increasing numbers of pupils engaging with each question and more pupils being able to accurately identify and correct inaccuracies. More students accurately answer questions at the end of the activity (either through hands up or in pupils' books) than at the start.

STRATEGY 7.2: Dictionaries and literacy mats

Two of the most underused resources in a school are dictionaries and literacy mats. Every lesson and every homework that needs a pupil to write accurately, every teacher and every parent should ensure the pupils have access to a dictionary and use them when doing their classwork or homework.

Outcome

At the end of the lesson, pupils will be able to understand, use and apply more words creatively and accurately in response to tasks and statements. This strategy makes the accuracy of usage clearer.

Use of the strategy: at the start and early stages of a topic

Whenever pupils are expected to write.

A useful strategy for also developing: knowledge and independent learning.

Resources

Dictionaries and literacy mats for the topic being taught.

How it works

- The teacher shows the pupils how to both find and accurately use previously unknown words in their work.

- This may initially be done verbally so pupils have an opportunity to experiment first and hear how the words are correctly pronounced.

- Keywords are displayed which are expected to be used accurately in context, verbally and in writing by the end of the lesson.

Continued on next page

■ The measure of success is in how many more words pupils understand and can use accurately in their work by the end of the lesson.

How will the teacher ensure learning has taken place?

Through setting high expectations that pupils must use a dictionary and/or literacy mat in a lesson, as well as ensuring pupils can increasingly use dictionaries and literacy mats successfully and accurately, eventually without any teacher intervention.

How will progress be seen to be made?

Progress in this activity will be visible through pupils meeting those high expectations as well as pupils more accurately spelling, reading, writing and using more words, phrases and terms in their work at the end of the task in hand (either through hands up, orally or in pupils' books) than at the start.

STRATEGY 7.3: Inspiring me, inspiring you

This activity is so motivational and can be applied to any subject. Like all lessons in language, getting the pupils to talk about the subject in question first is key to increasing their confidence in their accurate use of language, before writing anything.

Outcome

At the end of this activity, pupils will be able to produce a piece of accurate, persuasive writing that inspires others.

Timing of the activity

1–2 lessons or homework.

Resources

Inspirational quotes

How it works

■ The teacher presents quotes and speeches from inspirational people related to their subject.

■ Pupils analyse them and formulate success criteria as to what makes a great inspirational speech.

Continued on next page

- Using peer assessment, pupils develop arguments to justify points they make as to which is the best, most inspirational speech and why.

- Pupils then write their own inspirational speech.

- Pupils incorporate more keywords into their language and presentation, each time reviewing the presentation that other pupils are going to make.

- Applying the original success criteria to their own speeches, they self-assess and then peer assess the work.

- They then present and make their own speeches in front of a panel of pupils.

How will the teacher ensure learning has taken place?

Through ensuring pupils can increasingly use keywords accurately and correctly in an inspirational speech, eventually without any teacher intervention.

How will progress be seen to be made?

Progress in this activity will be visible through increasingly creative and accurate use of language and keywords, as well as the increasing length of speeches being written.

Year 9 example: My inspirational speech

Failure isn't a bad thing

Failure isn't necessarily bad because as normal human beings, we learn from them and that's fine.

When someone says you're a failure at something you shouldn't be sad about it; you should think about how you're going to prove them wrong.

It may take days, months or even years, but you will succeed one day.

"Failure is simply the opportunity to begin again, this time more intelligently".

We cope with failures every day.

It may be small, or it could be big, but we must try and try again.

Because, before you know it, you'll be telling people you learnt something new.

Albert Einstein said, "The person who never made a mistake, never tried anything new".

So, don't ever be afraid to try something new that interests you.

STRATEGY 7.4: Mini-whiteboards: accurately does it

This activity is a great one to use regularly with pupils who find it difficult to keep their books neat and their working out tidy. As a by-product, it also ensures their work is more accurate as a result.

Outcome

At the end of using this strategy, pupils will be able to produce a piece of accurate writing that is neat and tidy. It trains pupils to think/work answers out first and write later to avoid rushed writing and making mistakes in books. This will help develop more accurate writing and reduce mistakes, crossings out and misspelt words.

Use of the strategy: throughout a topic

Whenever pupils are expected to write or undertake calculations.

A useful strategy for also developing: skills and independent learning.

Resources

Books, mini-whiteboards, mini-whiteboard pens

How it works

- The teacher distributes a mini-whiteboard and pen to each (pair of) pupil(s).

- During the lesson, they are to be used to explore, experiment with spellings, ideas, calculations, sentences, trial, error and make mistakes.

- Only what is written in the books is the correct, accurate, final version.

How will the teacher ensure learning has taken place?

Through setting high expectations that there is to be no doodling, crossings out or inaccurate work in pupils' books. Through ensuring pupils understand and can use mini-whiteboards effectively and can increasingly write accurately and neatly in their books, eventually without the use of the mini-whiteboards.

How will progress be seen to be made?

Progress in this activity will be visible through pupils being able to meet those high expectations as well as more accurately and effectively use language verbally and in writing than at the start. Progress will be visible through increasingly accurate use of language and keywords, in speaking and writing, as well as an increased length of accurate writing evident in the book

STRATEGY 7.5: Do – review – improve

There's no better or more efficient way to get pupils to think and write on their own than by setting homework. This simple strategy allows them the scope to work independently at home and then check how well they have done in the classroom. Pure learning and plain and simple progress.

Outcome

By using this strategy, pupils will be able to understand, use and apply different words creatively and accurately in response to tasks and statements. This strategy makes the accuracy clearer.

Use of the strategy: at the end and then start of a lesson, throughout a topic.

Whenever pupils are expected to write and evaluate their work.

A useful strategy for also developing: knowledge, resilience and independent learning.

Resources

Homework task, library/use of the internet.

How it works

- The teacher sets a homework, for example an exam question for the pupils to do.

- The homework is then reviewed in the next lesson against a model answer, that's not perfect.

- The teacher gets the pupils to highlight a model answer against the assessment criteria.

- Pupils discuss in pairs and clarify how and why the model answer fits and fulfils the assessment criteria.

- Pupils apply the assessment criteria to their own answer completed for homework and self, or peer assess their homework.

- They then grade their own answer and confirm what was missing.

- They then discuss with a partner their assessed grade and what needs to be done to improve.

Continued on next page

How will the teacher ensure learning has taken place?

Through ensuring pupils can write answers independently that are increasingly accurate.

How will progress be seen to be made?

Progress in this activity will be visible through pupils more accurately spelling, reading, writing and using more words, phrases and terms in their work at the end of the task in hand (higher marks than would otherwise be the case, more accurate writing in response to the homework set in pupils' books) than at the start.

EXAMPLE: Geography

Homework: evaluate the impact of a named Transnational Corporation in a low-income country (9 marks)

Pupil: original answer completed as homework

Royal Dutch Shell has had a significant impact in Nigeria as it has created 65,000 jobs for people. Furthermore, Shell has invested in infrastructure and has spent money on the economy, creating a multiplier effect. Furthermore, Transnational Corporations (TNCs) often have charity in the countries they work in to help the local people. Shell has paid £20 billion in corporation taxes in 2013, and they have paid a lot of taxes in Nigeria.

On the contrary, Shell pays workers in Nigeria less than they would in the UK and working conditions are sometimes poor. Additionally, much of the profit generated goes abroad. TNCs have been accused by human rights abuses in the past and some TNCs have been known to use child labour. Shell have been accused of committing crimes against the Ogoni people in Nigeria. Furthermore, Shell have caused oil spills that damage sea life.

Overall, Shell has had a large economic benefit in Nigeria, as it has created many jobs. However, they have had many negative environmental effects. Controversially, people have been stealing oil illegally, and Shell and the government lots of money every year.

Teacher: model answer

Royal Dutch Shell has had a significant impact in Nigeria in several ways. Shell's economic impact in Nigeria has been overwhelmingly positive. Shell provides jobs for 65,000 Nigerians directly benefiting them and their families. Moreover, through the multiplier effect, the entire economy benefits. Shell is also responsible for extracting $30 billion (half of Nigeria's total oil revenue) worth of crude oil from Ogoniland. Through this, corporation tax and

Continued on next page

investment in infrastructure, it is evident that Shell has had an enormous impact on Nigeria and its economy and is arguably responsible for the fact that Nigeria now has the largest economy in Africa.

However, environmentally, it is a different story. The company has been responsible for oil spills across Nigeria, many of which hasn't cleared up. This has led to soil degradation and the loss of habitats and biodiversity. In Ogoniland where this issue was particularly bad, locals mounted peaceful protests. Following this, nine of the locals were executed and Shell has been accused of breaching human rights.

Overall, Shell has had a significant, positive impact as the environmental damage is more than offset by the positive economic impact. Though it should be noted that Shell profits massively from its operations in Nigeria and many of the 65,000 jobs are low paid with long working hours.

Notes from the pupil – additional marks that could have been gained through

The multiplier effect means that one person who earns more money and spends more money in the economy so that the economy has more money. This means that the government gets more money from taxes, so they can invest it in education. If people have a better education, then they can get higher paying jobs and therefore increase the money into the economy.

STRATEGY 7.6: Writing examinese

One of the biggest lessons in school (and in life) is that you must learn to sometimes modify your language and choose an appropriate response to suit your audience. So, it is in examinations. Unfortunately, it's not enough to just write an answer; pupils must write an answer that an examiner will accept. This is when we must teach the pupils how to speak the same language as the examiner in an exam and keep those marks coming.

Outcome

At the end of this strategy, pupils will be able to understand, use and apply more words, more accurately in response to the questions set. This strategy helps pupils apply their learning more accurately in an examination situation.

Use of the strategy: usually at the end of an activity or topic.

Whenever pupils are expected to write written answers worth more than 2 or 3 marks to an examination-style question, especially close to a test/ examination.

A useful strategy for also developing: skills, knowledge and application.

Continued on next page

Resources

Past examination papers/exemplar test papers.

How it works

The teacher gets the pupils to respond to examination-style questions with examination-style answers. Through translating and deconstructing exam-style questions into a language pupils can understand, the teacher then helps the pupils to answer the question and reconstruct the answer using keywords, phrases or structures that will gain marks with an examiner.

For example:

Question: Explain the impact of globalisation on the UK economy. [4 marks]

Step 1: Translate into English

Explain = Give reasons. "Because this happens...."

Impact = what happens, what's the result of....

Globalisation = a world-wide market and world-wide communication

UK economy = the finances of the UK

Question in English: How does the rest of the world and what they do affect the finances of the UK?

Step 2: Answer in English

A: Foreign companies can invest in the UK = more jobs

A: Imports from abroad = more choice of goods

A: More choice of foreign goods can lead to more money going out of the UK

A: If other countries are cheaper, the business will go there

Step 3: Translate back into Examinese

The impact of globalisation has led to direct investment in the UK from foreign companies abroad and, as a result, jobs in the UK have been created (1 mark). Affordable imports from TNCs give consumers in the UK more choice in the marketplace (1 mark), though the wealth created could go abroad to the TNC, if they don't invest further into the UK economy (1 mark). This could be especially true if the workforce, land and property rental is cheaper in other countries, compared to the UK (1 mark).

How will the teacher ensure learning has taken place?

Through ensuring pupils can increasingly accurately read, understand and answer the examination questions, eventually without any teacher intervention.

How will progress be seen to be made?

Progress in this activity will be visible through pupils more accurately spelling, reading, writing and using more words, phrases and terms in their work at the end of the task in hand (higher marks than would otherwise be the case, through hands up and more accurate writing in response to the examination questions in pupils' books) than at the start.

Implications for leaders: demonstrating impact

For the leader monitoring progress in accuracy, there are several tools available.

Quantitative measures: data analysis

Analysis of the assessment data is the clearest method of demonstrating impact (EEF, 2019c). Patterns in the data will emerge between individual pupils, small or large groups of pupils showing themes and variations in their assessment outcomes. A question that would arise for leaders is why are those patterns taking place? This may indicate that the transference of understanding in terms of what to do and how to produce accurate work, may be an issue.

Qualitative measures: book looks

A great starting place to see progress in accuracy is in pupils' books:

- Accurate spelling – being able to check for and see the accuracy of the spelling and the accuracy of spelling of increasingly more complex words throughout the exercise book.

- Accurate writing – being able to check for and see the accuracy of the writing with no (or increasingly less) crossings out, as pupils think more clearly and accurately.

- Accurate feedback – being able to check for and see the accuracy of the feedback and the responses to that feedback from peers or the teacher.

Book scrutiny – These initial findings can then be triangulated by looking in a number of pupils' books to see whether accuracy of work has been a focus by the teacher or not.

Qualitative measures: observations

Observations of the lesson will be able to indicate whether inaccuracies are picked up by the teacher during the lesson or not.

Qualitative measures: learning walks

Learning walks around a department or a school will identify patterns across several classes. Patterns may emerge related to accuracy that require praise and/or follow-up with a faculty or group of teachers.

Key questions

For teachers

1 How are you ensuring in your lessons that you are explicitly teaching pupils about both accuracy/inaccuracy and how to be more accurate?

2 How are you making best use of the resources at your disposal (dictionaries, literacy mats, mini-whiteboards, past exam papers) to improve the level of accuracy of the work of your pupils?

3 How regularly are you consciously transferring to the pupils the ability to lead their own learning and correct their own mistakes without you?

For leaders and governors

1 Have staff got the resources they need (dictionaries, literacy mats, mini-whiteboards, past exam papers) to enable pupils to work accurately and learn how to be accurate in what they do?

2 For the activities they create, are all staff clear about the success criteria for it to be completed accurately and do they have copies to go in the pupils' books?

3 What does the monitoring and tracking of pupil books tell you about how accurately pupils work?

4 What is the quality of the books in relation to marking, neatness, spelling and punctuation accuracy?

5 What patterns emerge from the data and what do those patterns tell you about how well pupils accurately work?

6 When you are observing lessons, how can you see progress being made in the lesson regarding accuracy?

7 When you are carrying out a learning walk of the school or a department, what evidence is there of pupils working increasingly accurately in what they do?

For parents

1 Where can you get a copy of the literacy mats/keyword banks used in your child's lessons, so you can support them more at home? Who is the person to contact?

2 What is the best dictionary and thesaurus for your child to use when doing their homework?

ENDNOTE

Progress in practice: lessons learnt in accuracy – Miss Pearson

Miss Pearson was my music teacher in secondary school. This story is about her and an incident which at the time was incredibly challenging but at the same time was incredibly empowering for me.

Looking back, this was a milestone moment and a real lesson in being accurate in what you do.

As a music pupil in Year 10 or Year 11, we were tasked with writing a piece of music for a group. I chose to write a piece of music for the school orchestra (why not?). Like everybody else in pre-computer days, I wrote music on manuscript paper with pencils and eraser. I completed my Opus 1 at home, which I was very keen to hear.

I had my orchestral piece written, all ready, with both the conductor's score and different parts for the different instruments in the orchestra. The school was fortunate to have a school orchestra on hand to try out my musical ideas. Miss Pearson was encouraging and happy to offer me two rehearsals to try out my ideas. When giving her the conductor's score and parts to pass out, she took them, looked at them, then passed them back to me. To my horror she said "This is your music. You conduct". After giving out the parts and a couple of minutes for each of the musicians to practice their part (and with a little conducting practice on my part), I nervously took to the podium and the piece began.

About 8–10 bars into the music, it became clear that something was not right. Someone was not playing the right notes, or they were playing the right notes but not necessarily in the right order.

I stopped the music.

Miss Pearson was smiling enigmatically. Clearly something wasn't right. I asked each section of the orchestra to play one at a time, listening to the strings, then woodwind, then brass, then percussion. The issue appeared to be in the brass section. When the situation was analysed further (through deft questioning on Miss Pearson's part), it transpired that the music for the brass instruments had been transposed in the wrong direction. Specifically, the French horn parts were a tone out. The implications were clear.

A slightly dismissive comment from Miss Pearson to the conductor with a "Well, you'll just have to take the whole lot away, re-write the brass parts and come back next week" left me crestfallen.

When I got home, I was annoyed with myself. I thought I'd covered every eventuality but clearly not. I set to work and re-wrote (this time accurately) the French horn parts in the orchestral score and the parts for the instruments (a couple of hours work) and reappeared the following week and the following rehearsal with the new score.

Continued on next page

In all honesty, I was feeling sick. Everyone had been present the previous week and witnessed my mistake very publicly. Again, I gave out the parts for the orchestra to practice, took to the podium and took the baton handed to me by the enigmatically smiling Miss Pearson.

The music started and 8–10 bars in, magically, everything worked! We got to the end of the piece and a round of applause from the band brought tears to my eyes and a "Well done" from a beaming Miss Pearson. I had corrected my mistake, had learnt the theoretical and practical aspects of transposition and had effectively learnt my lesson.

For any pupil, writing is arguably one of the most difficult and complex activities you can do. That this was one of the most difficult, complex challenges for a pupil, was down to the courage and talent of a music teacher who pointed to the sky and encouraged and supported her pupil to reach for it. This was after all about developing my skill as a musician.

This instance was also about accuracy – accuracy of knowledge. It was not necessary to question me about the whys and wherefores of my choices. In terms of the teaching, Miss Pearson had clearly considered what would be the best way for the pupil to learn to be more accurate – in theory or in practice? By experience in a small experimental situation, or in theory at a desk?

The fact that I am writing this now, decades later, indicates it was a lesson most effectively learned.

At the time, it made me feel very challenged, but it also made me feel empowered, especially as I was one of the few pupils who was trying out this challenge. I can only guess and hope that it made her proud that the activity worked so well.

In a nutshell, with regard to accuracy, teachers should always consider the best ways for pupils to make and learn from their mistakes – in theory or in practice.

Sometimes the best lessons are learnt by getting things wrong, but then very quickly learning the lesson and putting things right.

8 Progress in the lesson: resilience

Progress in resilience plain and simple:

Progress in resilience lies in the pupil being able to more successfully meet the challenges in their work and, as a result, work for longer.

How are the challenges ahead to be met, if not with resilience?

In this chapter we will cover:

- What we mean by resilience
- Consciously teaching resilience
- Enabling pupils to be more resilient
- Teaching resilience in practice: activities and strategies
- Implications for leaders on resilience
- Questions to help further understand and improve resilience

Introduction

The fourth measure of progress in the classroom to discuss is resilience, for example to be able to write knowledgeably and accurately for longer.

Resilience is about the pupil's ability to face and overcome the problems and challenges they face and, as a result, continue to make progress in their work; in other words, work more effectively and for longer.

From a teacher's perspective, there is an old Chinese proverb which summarises this clearly and simply:"*Give* someone a fish, and you feed them for a day. *Teach* someone to fish, and you feed them for a lifetime".This chapter is therefore not about how *teachers can manage* the challenges presented by their pupils (and pupils can be challenging!) but about *teaching pupils how to manage* and overcome those challenges themselves and as a result work more successfully for longer.

The focus of this chapter is to make clear the progress in learning related to resilience. That is the incremental improvements in solving problems and ensuring the quantity of work completed increases: more work, more writing, being able to continue activities for longer and being able to discuss, think creatively and solve problems. Thus, the implication for teaching is about creating and presenting pupils with incremental challenges and enabling pupils to work out their own solutions and successfully overcome those challenges.

The reason for this focus is that, like teaching accuracy, there can be too little emphasis by the teacher on helping and teaching pupils how to manage the challenges they are going to face. As a result, the teacher can spend a huge amount of time going around the class dealing with the individual student issues and metaphorically giving them a fish, rather than teaching them how to manage their challenges, teaching them how to fish.

What we mean by progress in resilience

MEASURE OF PROGRESS: THE ABILITY TO BE RESILIENT

FROM THE TEACHER	FROM THE PUPIL
NUMEROUS OPPORTUNITIES TO BE RESILIENT	INCREASED PRACTICE AT BEING RESILIENT
CLEARER EXPLANATIONS OF RESILIENCE	GREATER UNDERSTANDING OF RESILIENCE
MORE FEEDBACK ON PUPIL RESILIENCE	MORE CONFIDENT AT BEING RESILIENT
INCREMENTALLY DIFFICULT CHALLENGES SET	OPPORTUNITIES TO PRACTICE BEING MORE RESILIENT

This fourth measure of progress and a different measure to skill, knowledge and accuracy is the degree of resilience with which a pupil faces challenges when learning. This has a set of different measures and criteria, in the sense that a skill is an active, demonstrable measure. Something is harder, more complex. Similarly, knowledge is a more intangible measure, less demonstrable. Pupils either know something or they don't, they know more, or they don't. This fourth measure, resilience, is very different in that it focuses on helping pupils to overcome the issues or problems they face. This therefore requires a different teaching technique. A technique which is about teaching problem-solving and perseverance.

When we look for a specific definition of resilience, the dictionary defines it as "the <u>ability</u> to be <u>happy</u>, or <u>successful</u> after something <u>difficult</u> or <u>bad</u> has <u>happened</u>". Researchers define it as "the process of effectively negotiating, adapting to, or managing significant sources of stress or trauma" (Windle, 2011). In the case of the pupil, this would equate to the pupil's ability to be successful in both meeting and working through the challenges set by the teacher. A second definition by the dictionary "the <u>ability</u> of a <u>substance</u> to <u>return</u> to <u>its</u> <u>usual</u> <u>shape</u> after being <u>bent</u>, <u>stretched</u>, or <u>pressed</u>" suggests a short period of stress, of stretching and returning to a previous state. Again, in the case of the pupil, this suggests a short period of being stretched and stressed and then returning to a more relaxed state of mind.

> The measure for resilience is therefore about how challenging the activities are and the pupil's ability to successfully manage and overcome those challenges, subsequently able to work harder and for longer.

What the research says about the teaching and learning of resilience

In addition to what the research says about progress in general, as outlined in Chapter 3, there are a couple of points raised specifically in the research about progress related to resilience.

With researchers being unclear as to what defines resilience (Windle, 2011, Chmitorz et al., 2018), I'd like to be as clear as I can be from the outset. Resilience is both a trait in a person and a dynamic process in a person's behaviour which can change over time: in other words, a skill (PSHE Association, 2017).

Resilience then, like a skill, can be taught so that pupils improve and develop their resilience over time and, as a result, make more progress (Hanson, 2004, Windle, 2011, PSHE Association, 2017, Chmitorz et al., 2018). However, whilst there are a number of research studies that measure resilience, or give guidance to support pupils to be more resilient (Rosenshine, 1986, Muijs and Reynolds, 2017), there is little research into what interventions are effective in supporting and improving resilience as a skill (Chmitorz, et al., 2018).

Learning to be resilient is important. In the next 20 years, we are going to see further increases in technology and globalisation in the workplace and, as a result, pupils being able to be adaptable, resilient and resourceful are key skills to future success in the marketplace (UKCES, 2014).

Alongside optimism and self-control, resilience can be central in helping pupils make improved progress (Hanson, 2004, Tough, 2012), with a direct link between a pupil's academic attainment and high levels of resilience (Hanson, 2004). Similarly, charisma and the ability to be compassionate, explain work clearly and help pupils understand, are qualities of the very best teachers (Coates, 2015, p.85, Tomsett, 2015, p.14).

In one of the few pieces of research on resilience, Rook et al. (2018) present their athlete framework for workplace resilience which recommends four ways in which the teacher can support and develop a pupil's resilience: help them be tolerant with the experience of challenge; increase their intellectual capacity to accept challenge; help them cope with the physical process of dealing with the challenge and adapt as necessary (Rook, 2018).

Resilience is about adjusting to challenge and managing to bounce back when it happens. It occurs in several ways in a school: as academic resilience in a pupil's work and as emotional resilience in a pupil's relationships with others. Successful pupils have high levels of persistence and resilience, able to plan how to overcome a problem; unsuccessful pupils do not (EEF, 2019d).

The focus of the book in relation to this is in helping pupils with their academic resilience. Pupils who have previously suffered stress or trauma may not respond well to challenge in class. As a result, the teacher helping them be more resilient and manage their stress effectively in these situations is key. This would be especially true for some pupils with behavioural needs or who are particularly challenging in class (Windle, 2011, Rook et al., 2018). As a result, PSHE is well suited as a subject to help pupils develop their understanding of resilience (PSHE Association, 2017). As Gill Windle (2011) says, "the capacity for 'ordinary magic' and the opportunity for positive adaptation should be an option for everyone".

Consciously teaching resilience: how resilience is taught

Progress in resilience requires much patience from the teacher.

From a starting point of assuming that pupils can't show much resilience in their work, much explanation and demonstration is needed by the teacher at the start. Managing this adeptly through effective routines and a consistently helpful, approachable teaching manner early on will get the pupils quickly through an important learning stage that can be reinforced and used well in subsequent lessons.

As such, being resilient is a skill that can be trained.

Resilience is the pupil's ability to be able to persevere with their work, to not stop, to keep going, to not let distractions and difficulties get in the way of completing the work to the expected standard.

Activities and strategies that promote progress in resilience

This section offers a range of strategies and activities that promote progress in resilience. As with the previous activities and strategies related to skills, knowledge and accuracy, they should be used when the situation requires them. *It is for the teacher to use their professional judgement in deciding when the best time is to apply them.*

The strategies and activities are ordered in a suggested succedent order. The strategies and activities at the start being recommended for use at the start of a lesson or topic and the strategies and activities at the end, being useful at the end of a lesson or topic.

As with earlier activities and strategies, many of them may not be new to the reader. However, the value of each strategy lies in promoting progress in a particular area and suggesting a timing when the strategy or activity is likely to be most effective.

Again, for experienced teachers, this section provides several recommendations which you can use to refresh your memory of strategies and activities that you may have used in the past and maybe need to bring back again to the fore. The strategies and activities will also provide confirmation that in already doing these strategies and activities with your classes confirms the good practice in your own choice of teaching strategies.

For less experienced teachers, I hope you find this section useful and full of easy-to-apply ideas that will help you and your classes experience far more progress being made in a shorter duration of time with respect to your students' resilience.

An affirmation

Be more resilient

Face and overcome the distractions that come along to take away your time, energy and concentration, and in doing so

Make progress

It's OK

To feel frustrated

To make mistakes

To take time to think

To take time to find the answer

To talk through a way forward with a friend.

For every question, there is an answer.

For every problem, there is a solution.

STRATEGY 8.1: Metacognition – learning to solve problems

This strategy sets the context and prepares pupils for the challenges ahead. It is a key method by which teachers can help pupils be open and ready to learn the lessons that are to follow.

Outcome

The outcome is for every pupil to be able to master the challenges that face them in the activity/lesson/topic.

Use of the strategy: at the start of a lesson/activity and topic

At the start of a lesson/activity/topic when the pupils are about to face a new/ significant challenge.

A useful strategy for also developing: skills.

How it works

■ The rule at the start is "all hands up". Whenever a teacher asks a question and asks for a response, all hands must go up. Some may have the answer, others may have a question, others may have an observation. Either way, all responses are accepted.

Continued on next page

■ The teacher presents the activity, explains the challenges the pupil is going to face in the activity/topic and asks them to assess the risks and identify their strengths and weaknesses in facing/managing each one.

■ The teacher then asks the pupils to plan how they are going to attempt the activity and overcome any issues as they arise will help the pupil clarify their actions and response. Having a poster of top tips displayed to help pupils plan and make the best choices, will also help the pupils understand how to build their resilience.

■ Once the activity has been completed, having some reflection time as to how well the strategies worked, will help strengthen the pupils' understanding of how to be more resilient and more effective at problem-solving in the future.

How will the teacher ensure learning has taken place?

Through the reflective, informed and accurate responses to the question posed "If you find this challenging, how are you going to work through those challenges?"

How will progress be seen to be made?

Through more pupils being more able to start and continue with an activity and not give up.

STRATEGY 8.2: knowing what to do and how to do it

A second early challenge for pupils is where the pupil doesn't know what to do in an activity, or doesn't understand how to do it, for a whole host of reasons. This strategy should be done routinely to support pupils and ensure the teacher's instructions have been clear and easily understood.

Outcome

By the end of this strategy, pupils are clear about what to do, how to do it and can get on with the work set. The teacher also understands who might need extra support as a result.

Use of the strategy: at the start of an activity

Useful during an activity when a pupil (or class) is not on task.

A useful strategy for also developing: listening skills.

Continued on next page

Sign of resilience being needed

When a pupil is doing anything other than what they are supposed to do.

How it works

- Once a task or activity has been set, the teacher asks pupils if:

1 They understand what to do to successfully complete the activity and

2 They understand how to do the work to successfully complete the activity.

■ Should none/some of the class put their hands up, the teacher needs to re-visit the instructions.

■ Should most/all of the class put their hands up, the teacher can then follow up with one or two individuals at random to cross-check the pupils know what to do and how to do it.

How will the teacher ensure learning has taken place?

Through clear instructions and strong behaviour management. Through the accurate responses to the questions posed.

How will progress be seen to be made?

Through more pupils being more able to start and continue with an activity and not give up.

STRATEGY 8.3: Getting the pupils to try

This is the first significant challenge that usually presents itself for any teacher; being faced with a pupil (or group of pupils) who can't/won't do the task set. This strategy helps the teacher and the pupil get started on the road to progress.

Outcome

By the end of this strategy, pupils should be able to try the work set.

Use of the strategy: during a lesson/activity

Useful at the very start of an activity when a pupil is refusing to do the work set.

A useful strategy for also developing: skills, independent learning.

Continued on next page

How it works

- The teacher explains to the class why the topic being taught is important (to them), how they are going to benefit from studying this topic and outlines the activities and how pupils are going to be able to engage with them and see their skills/knowledge improve.

- Once the class are working, the teacher should follow up with individuals who are struggling to engage.

- With the individual, the teacher explains that they are going to do one or two activities with the pupil watching, they do one or two activities together and then one or two with the pupil doing the activity on their own.

- If the pupil is reluctant, the teacher should give an opportunity for the pupil to voice their fears or concerns and then address them.

- The teacher then does one or two activities talking out loud as to how they are doing it, with the pupil watching. This is followed by starting the next activity but getting the pupil to finish it off. Finally, the last activity is getting the pupil to start and finish the activity with the teacher watching.

- The pupil should now be able to do the activity themselves. Getting another pupil to support also helps embed the start.

How will the teacher ensure learning has taken place?

Through clear instructions, adept problem-solving and strong behaviour management. Through carefully managed support and ensuring the student tries to complete the work set.

How will progress be seen to be made?

When a pupil is more able to try an activity and not give up straight away.

STRATEGY 8.4: "Show me that was skill, not luck!"

Another significant challenge that faces most teachers at the start of a new project is when the pupil gives up after barely starting. Here, the pupil has tried and understands what to do and how to do the task in hand but doesn't necessarily have all the skills needed to complete the task set.

Continued on next page

Outcome

By the end of this strategy pupils are more confident about what to do, how to do it and able to complete the work set.

Use of the strategy: during an activity

Useful during an activity when a pupil is off task or doing the task in the wrong way.

A useful strategy for also developing: skills, independent learning.

How it works

- This is different from the previous strategy in that the pupil has started but lacks confidence. The strategy is therefore about checking and clarifying for the pupil what needs to be done and giving them the clarification and confidence to do it.

- The teacher asks the pupil: What needs to be done and if they understand how to do it.

- If the answer is "No", then the teacher revisits this.

- If the answer is "Yes", then the teacher asks the pupil to show them the activity.

- Here the teacher is looking for errors or hesitation.

- If the pupil shows hesitation, this needs encouraging and confidence building. If there is inaccuracy, this needs correcting with a few short exercises to help, if necessary.

- The teacher asks the pupils to then do a similar exercise saying, "Show me that was skill and not just luck".

- The pupil repeats an exercise and should this time be able to more confidently do it on their own.

How will the teacher ensure learning has taken place?

Through clear instructions, adept problem-solving and strong behaviour management. Through carefully managed support and ensuring the student tries to complete the work set.

How will progress be seen to be made?

When a pupil is more confident and able to continue with an activity and not give up.

STRATEGY 8.5: Reinforcing confidence

Towards the end of a topic, or especially as pupils get older and approach the time they are moving key stage, pupils tend to know what they are doing, they just need reassurance. At this stage, it's time to literally let go and let them sort it out for themselves. This is where the teacher must be cruel to be kind, in a constructive, supportive, albeit seemingly unsupportive way.

Outcome

Pupils are more confident about what to do, how to do it and able to complete the work set independently.

Use of the strategy: during and towards the end of an activity

Useful during an activity when a pupil is requiring attention but has been working well.

A useful strategy for also developing: independent learning.

Sign of resilience being needed

The pupil needing regular reassurance about what they are doing.

Teacher response

The teacher should reassure the pupil they are there and available, but subtly and politely leave the pupil to realise they are able to manage the activity without the help of the teacher.

How it works

■ The teaching strategy that helps here is to not respond to the pupil's needs straight away.

■ This allows the pupil time to work through any anxieties and provide their own reassurance that they do know what to do.

■ The teacher then visits other pupils nearby and sees the pupil in question later to check that they have managed to successfully solve their problems without the input of the teacher. In this way pupils must do the work on their own and must be confident in what they are doing.

■ The teacher then revisits the student to congratulate them on showing the required resilience.

Continued on next page

How will the teacher ensure learning has taken place?

Through enabling students to recognise that they have the resilience to manage their challenges.

How will progress be seen to be made?

When a pupil is more confident in their work and able to continue without needing the reassurance of the teacher.

STRATEGY 8.6: Strengthening working at pace – speed

When we are working slowly (or slower than we ought), sometimes we do not know that there are quicker ways to do something, or we haven't needed to do something quickly before and as a result have got into slow habits. In this case, the pupil knows what to do and is confident in what they are doing. The issue here is that they need to put more energy and effort into doing it and being confident at working at a faster pace.

Outcome

Pupils are more confident that they can work at a faster pace than they would otherwise have done.

Use of the strategy: in the middle of an activity/topic

Useful when pupils are working too slowly and getting behind in their work.

A useful strategy for also developing: skills and accuracy.

Sign of resilience being needed

Pupils don't complete all the work set in time.

Teacher response

The teacher should reduce the time taken to complete the same number of activities. As a result, the pupils work faster but with no reduction in the quality of their work.

How it works

■ The teacher sets timed activities to help cover more curriculum, more quickly and build stamina. For example, first setting fifteen minutes to do three activities, then setting ten minutes to do three similar activities, followed by setting eight minutes to do a further three similar activities.

Continued on next page

■ This incrementally helps build pupil confidence in working at *pace*, strengthening their stamina and resilience in securing similar amounts of work completed *in less time*.

How will the teacher ensure learning has taken place?

By clarifying the skills needed to complete the task and checking the accuracy of the work completed whilst reducing the amount of time set.

How will progress be seen to be made?

When pupils are more confident in their work and able to complete the same amount of work in a shorter period of time.

STRATEGY 8.7: Strengthening working at pace – stamina

We all know the feeling of giving up, paying less attention to something because either our brain is saturated with too much information, or we just aren't used to using our brains so much in such a space of time. As a result, we give up, needing time out from our brains feeling overloaded. This isn't a question of not knowing what to do, nor working for long enough. The issue here is in being able to process the information and the work, in the time available.

Outcome

Pupils are more confident that they can complete more work in the same amount of time than they would otherwise have done.

Use of the strategy: in the middle of a lesson/later in a topic

Useful when pupils are not completing enough work in the time set and getting behind in their work.

A useful strategy for also developing: skills and accuracy.

Sign of resilience being needed

Pupils don't complete all the work set in time.

Teacher response

The teacher should maintain the time taken to complete more activities. As a result, the pupils work harder but with no reduction in the quality of their work.

Continued on next page

How it works

- The teacher sets timed activities to help cover more curriculum, more quickly and build stamina.

- For example, first setting ten minutes to do three activities, then setting ten minutes to do four similar activities, followed by setting ten minutes to do a further five similar activities.

- This incrementally helps build pupil stamina in working at *pace*, strengthening their stamina and resilience in securing *larger amounts of work* completed in a similar time.

How will the teacher ensure learning has taken place?

By clarifying the skills needed to complete the task and checking the accuracy of the work completed whilst increasing the amount of work set.

How will progress be seen to be made?

When pupils are more confident in their work and able to complete more work in the same amount of time than they had done previously.

Implications for leaders: demonstrating impact

For the leader monitoring progress in resilience, there are several tools available.

Quantitative measures: data analysis

Firstly, data tracking sheets should show shorter, easier tests and assessments being given at the start of the year (Level 1 test/10) with tests and assessments later in the year being longer and more difficult (Level 4 test/40). Here, the leader can clearly see that more and more difficult learning is being tested and as a result of increased challenge, pupils must show greater resilience in their work.

Secondly, carrying out a question analysis as to how many pupils completed each question and completed the test paper in the set time will indicate not only how much pupils may or may not know but also how resilient they were in exam conditions. This will help leaders identify learning and resilience issues and therefore modify their teaching and their courses as a result.

Qualitative measures: book looks

Completion of work: All work in the books is complete, or increasingly complete. This shows that the pupil can overcome issues and understand and complete the work set.

Clarity of work: There is no (or decreasing) graffiti or doodles in a pupil's book. This shows that the pupil is on task and concentrating in class. Evidence of graffiti or doodles in books suggests the pupils are either bored and are not being sufficiently challenged, or don't understand what to do, don't have the resilience to complete the work and need further support. Either way, this is an issue to be addressed.

Qualitative measures: observations

Observations of a lesson will be able to indicate whether the teacher is consciously teaching pupils to be resilient, indicated by how many pupils are on task and can continue to be on task as the lesson progresses.

Qualitative measures: learning walks

Learning walks will identify patterns across several classes and indicate the mindset of a group of teachers. If there is a mindset of not focusing on resilience across several lessons or subjects, indicated by a number of pupils being off task or struggling with their work, then a learning walk around a faculty or the school will indicate whether there is a need to address resilience collectively with staff through Continuing Professional Development, or collectively with pupils through an assembly.

Key questions

For teachers

1 How are you ensuring in your lessons that you are explicitly teaching pupils about resilience and how to be more resilient?

2 How are you ensuring in your lessons that you are explicitly teaching pupils to know how to successfully solve problems themselves and work through their own challenges?

3 How are you making best use of the activities to set increasingly difficult challenges to increase the level of resilience in your pupils?

4 How regularly are you consciously transferring to the pupils the ability to lead their own learning and be resilient without you?

For leaders and governors

1 Are all staff clear about what resilience is and how pupils demonstrate resilience in their lessons?

2 Do leaders and staff understand how to teach and enable pupils to be increasingly resilient in their subject areas?

3 What does the monitoring and tracking of pupil books tell you about how resilient pupils are in their work?

4 What is the quality of the books in relation to graffiti, completed work and their overall tidiness?

5 What patterns emerge from the data and what does that tell you about how resilient pupils are in their work?

6 When you are observing lessons, how can you see progress in the pupils working with resilience?

7 When you are carrying out a learning walk of the school or a department, what evidence is there of pupils working with increasing resilience in what they do?

8 How well does the PSHE programme explicitly and effectively develop every pupil's resilience?

For parents

1 What does the school recommend you can do as a parent to help improve your child's resilience with their homework?

2 What questions can you ask your child to help them have a clearer understanding of the challenges they are facing with their schoolwork, who to talk to and how to work through them?

ENDNOTE

Progress in practice: a crash course in resilience

One year on holiday, after climbing more than enough mountains, I decided that it would be a good idea to do something different and so signed myself and my other half up for some white-water rafting. The local area was famous for it, and so if there was anywhere to learn how to white-water raft, this was it.

The initial training at the start was disconcerting, to say the least. Following a safety talk by the boat's captain and his team of one, we were each kitted out with rubber suit, helmet, lifejacket and paddle. After changing, we were then invited into the boat (on dry land) to practice drill. For the best part of half an hour in the boat (on dry land), we were shouted at by the instructor. "Left!" (sat on the left, I pretend to paddle like mad). "Right!" (sat on the right, my other half pretends to paddle like mad). "Ahead!" (we both pretend to paddle like mad). All the while these commands were flying, there were accompanying hand gestures, in case we missed his bellows in the maelstrom of whirling water (incomprehensible at this moment given that we were on dry land). A group of locals walking past, stop, giggle and point at us, in what I can only assume is a comical scene – two life jacketed, helmeted rubber suits being shouted at, paddling like mad on dry land.

After a few final instructions (what to do if the boat overturns, what to do if someone falls overboard and to never, *never* lose a paddle), our instructor was eventually happy that we were ready to go.

The moment arrived when we had to put the boat into the water and get in. The water at this point was calm and like an English river, a steadily flowing pastoral idyll. We got into the boat and started paddling, enjoying the scenery and the relaxing speed. Within ten minutes, the rapids started and what had been a slow, calm and relaxed cruise turned very quickly to a fast, challenging, paddle-for-your-life. The fast, churning water kept hurling us directly at enormous boulders, then sending us through the narrowest of gaps, as at every turn we tried to escape imminent collision and danger. The instructions and gesticulations were coming thick and fast. The gradient dropped further. The water turned into cascades: a bucking herd of wild white horses. There was no opportunity to give up. There was no opportunity to disengage, to say I can't do this, take a breather, to correct, strengthen, or build up confidence. We had to simply be resilient and paddle for our lives.

Eventually, of course, the torrent subsided, a bridge came into view and we pulled in. At the end of the experience, we were both exhilarated and exhausted. We had experienced one of the best boat rides of our lives.

We had also experienced a very short but very intense lesson in resilience.

9 Progress in the lesson: independent learning

Progress in independence plain and simple:

Progress in independent learning is in the pupil being able to work successfully for longer on their own.

Is this not the goal of education, for pupils to succeed independently?

In this chapter, we will cover:

- What we mean by independence in learning
- Consciously teaching independent learning
- Enabling pupils to be more independent learners
- Modelling independence in learning including reading
- Teaching independent learning in practice: activities and strategies
- Implications for leaders on independence in learning
- Questions to help further understand and improve independence in learning

Introduction

The fifth progress measure in the classroom to discuss is independent learning, for example to be able to write knowledgeably and accurately, for longer, on your own.

This chapter focuses on the pupil's ability to learn on their own, without the help of other adults such as teachers or parents. The aim of this chapter is to make clear how teachers can teach, and pupils make progress in independent learning. It is in the incremental improvements in the pupil's ability to consolidate all the areas we have covered and have the wherewithal to do it on their own.

In the classroom, when teaching pupils how to be more independent in their learning, it is important that pupils are given by the teacher, the explicit opportunity to work independently; to teach pupils not just how to do the task in hand, but to create opportunities for them to do it themselves.

What we mean by progress in independent learning

MEASURE OF PROGRESS: THE ABILITY TO LEARN INDEPENDENTLY

The three activities that enable independent learning are:

Activity	Initiative to work	Teacher presence	Pupil independence
Classwork	Teacher directed	Teacher present	Pupil works on own or with others
Homework	Teacher directed	Teacher absent	Pupil works on own
Independent work	Pupil directed	Teacher absent	Pupil works on own

This fifth and final measure of progress and a different measure to skill, knowledge, accuracy and resilience is the degree of independence with which a pupil can work. This has a set of different measures and criteria as can be seen in the table above.

As regards classwork, the teacher sets the work and dictates how much the pupil completes the work in class independently. It may be that the teacher allows pupils to work together, for example, peer assessing each other's work, or it may be necessary for the pupils to work on their own. Thus, independent learning can take place within a lesson, but this is directed by the teacher and has the teacher present to monitor and ensure that the quality of pupil work meets the expected standard. Hence, this first activity that enables independent learning is classwork. This allows a level of monitored independence where the pupil demonstrates in the class an increasing ability to work successfully and independently.

As a follow-up, or in preparation for the next lesson, the teacher can set homework for the pupil to complete outside the classroom. This incrementally increases the amount of independence with which a pupil works.

Homework, whilst being initiated and directed by the teacher for completion and with the success criteria shared, the pupil must complete it without the teacher present and as such, must be able to understand and successfully complete the work set, to the required standard, without any additional teacher support or input. Hence, a second activity that enables independent learning is homework.

A third activity that enables progress in independent learning is the pupil's ability to initiate and complete the learning for themselves. Here, the teacher may initiate the learning and set the success criteria for it, but it is for the pupil to research and find the information for themselves. This allows the pupil most freedom and independence to study (making the learning more personalised and as a result more memorable and effective) and at the same time ensures it meets the set criteria for a piece of successful research.

Thus, progress in independent learning is about incremental increases in pupil independence; from teacher led moving to pupil led; from working as a class to working as a group; to working in pairs to pupils successfully working on their own.

What the research says about the teaching and learning of independent learning

In addition to what the research says about progress in general, as outlined in Chapter 3, there are a couple of points raised in the research specifically about progress related to independent learning.

The research is clear that independent learning without explicit guidance is less effective than if it has explicit guidance (Kirschner, 2006). Making guidance explicit as to how pupils learn independently will help improve their learning and progress. If it is not explicit, as well as it being ineffective, the work runs the risk of being inaccurate through being misunderstood on the part of the pupil.

> The participation of pupils in explicit discussion of each of the steps is seen as essential, and part of the way pupils may come to understand the logic of learning, thus functioning better as independent learners.
>
> (Swann, 1988, p. 311)

In addition, group work is a great way to foster independent learning (Coates, 2015, p.93) and helps aid progress (Solomon, 2015).

Finally, whilst the empirical research as to how effective homework is may be ambiguous (Muijs and Reynolds, 2017), the professional research says that homework adds about five months more progress to a pupils' learning (EEF, 2019b).

What is clear from the research is that where homework is most effective, it is planned and focused. It is also clear that it is not the *quantity* of homework set, but the *quality* of it that counts. Thus, the homework policy, programmes of study and schemes of work should be explicit in what homework should be set and when.

Recommendations:

✓ Homework must be clear as to what must be included for it to be completed successfully.

✓ Homework can be set ahead of a lesson for pupils to read, understand and prepare key work ahead of the lesson.

✓ Homework can be set ahead of or after a lesson but always incorporating different levels of challenge.

✓ Homework can be set after a lesson for pupils to recap and review what's been learnt, reinforcing the learning that has taken place. This may be useful for pupils that need to catch up.

✓ Homework can be set after a set of lessons for the pupil to revise their work ahead of a test being set in the next lesson.

✓ Whenever the homework is set, it must always be meaningful and referred to in the next lesson.

✓ Homework should not be set as a research project, unless it has clear success criteria. The research is clear that this type of homework can be too unstructured and as a result, pupils do not learn or make as much progress as with other more structured independent learning activities.

Consciously teaching independent learning: how independent study is taught

> Independent learning requires a different teaching technique to the others. Teaching independent learning not only creates opportunities for pupils to learn on their own but being explicit with the success criteria enables pupils to learn on their own successfully.

> Opportunity + Success Criteria = Successful Independent Learning

Setting homework or independent study creates the opportunity; sharing the success criteria will go some way to enabling the pupils to successfully learn independently, as Swann states "...in making explicit how pupils learn independently, will help improve their learning and progress" (Swann, 1988). In terms of teaching in the classroom, the teacher needs to share the success criteria at the start of the lesson and then consciously, incrementally remove any scaffolding during the lesson, so that by the end of the lesson, the pupil can work successfully and completely on their own.

Activities and strategies that promote progress in independent learning

This section offers a range of strategies and activities that promote progress in independent learning. As with the previous activities and strategies related to skills, knowledge, accuracy and resilience, they should be used when the situation requires them. *It is for the teacher to use their professional judgement in deciding when the best time is to apply them.*

Progress in independent learning requires the teacher to consciously let go, in a structured way. Managing this adeptly through organised, incrementally independent activities and homework early on will move the pupils quickly through an important learning stage that can be reinforced and used well in subsequent lessons.

As with earlier activities and strategies, many of these may not be new to the reader. However, the value of each strategy lies in promoting progress in a particular area and suggesting a timing when the strategy is likely to be most effective.

Again, for experienced teachers, this section provides several recommendations which you can use to refresh your memory of strategies and activities that you used in the past and possibly need to bring back again to the fore. The strategies and activities will also provide confirmation that in already doing these strategies and activities with your classes confirms the good practice your own choice of teaching strategies.

For less experienced teachers, I hope you find this section useful and full of easy-to-apply ideas that will help you and your classes see far more progress being made in a shorter duration of time with respect to independent learning.

MINI-STRATEGY 9.1: De-scaffolding

Success criteria:

Pupils can complete the work set without the teacher.

How it works:

- Start the lesson with simple examples and clear explanations, both given by the teacher.
- With subsequent examples, the teacher draws out explanations from the pupils.
- Any issues that arise are discussed and solutions found.
- With further subsequent examples, the pupils are able to work through them and deal with any issues on their own.

MINI-STRATEGY 9.2: Un-prompted progress

Success criteria

Pupils can successfully respond to the tasks set without prompts from the teacher.

How it works

- The teacher gives pupils numerous prompts at the start of the lesson, for example, giving the pupils sentence stems, missing words sentences or keywords that need to be used to help pupils structure their answers.
- Explaining what the prompts do and requiring pupils to create their own prompts, incrementally transfers the creation of the prompts and the ability to work independently, more on to the pupils.
- By the end of the lesson, the teacher should be able to not use any prompts and the pupils can work as successfully, providing their own prompts and able to work successfully on their own.

STRATEGY 9.3: Homework

Whilst the government may not make homework a statutory activity for schools, and Ofsted may not be interested in inspecting it, according to the Education Endowment Foundation (2019b), homework can provide cheaply on average, an additional five months progress to a child's learning over a year. What other reason is there for a teacher to not set homework every week? As the pupils are more likely to be more knowledgeable as a result of doing their homework, all schools should be putting homework high on their agenda.

Secondly, schools (and parents) literally spend millions of pounds on interventions so that the pupils are more likely to be guaranteed to pass their exams. Setting more homework, more frequently and sharing with the pupils the success criteria for their homework will help reduce the amount of time teachers have to stay back after school and provide costly interventions. Schools having a clear, robust and rigorously enforced homework policy here is key.

Lastly, schools will literally have thousands of fewer pupils in detentions if they make the success criteria explicit to pupils when setting homework. I have had more conversations than I care to mention with aggravated pupils and even more aggravated parents about pupils having completed a homework (satisfactorily in their view) only to be given a detention because it wasn't good enough. How is the pupil or the parent to know this, if the teacher is not explicit about it from the start?

Thus, a plea: Teachers, please ensure your homework has clear success criteria so we reduce the number of pupils being kept back after school and therefore make everyone's lives that little bit easier!

MINI-STRATEGY 9.4: Re-grouping

Success criteria

By the end of the lesson, the pupils can successfully work on their own.

How it works

- At the start of the lesson, the teacher questions or completes a task with the whole class.
- Each subsequent activity has an increasingly smaller number of pupils in the group, for example, working in groups of eight, then four, then in pairs.
- Eventually, the pupils work on their own.
- This strategy incrementally decreases the number of pupils working together and therefore increases the level of independent learning taking place in the classroom.

MINI-STRATEGY 9.5: Pupil talk

Success criteria

By the end of the lesson, the pupils can successfully work in silence.

How it works

- At the start of the lesson, the teacher allows whole class discussion on a topic.
- Each subsequent activity has pupils having an increasingly smaller number of pupils with whom they can talk and discuss their work, for example, in fours, then in pairs.
- Eventually, the pupils must work in silence.
- This strategy incrementally decreases the number of pupils discussing working together and therefore increases the level of independent work taking place in the classroom.

MINI-STRATEGY 9.6: Reading programmes

Reading is unnatural, takes a long time to develop, but is the most important skill we can learn independently (Lyon, 1998). It is also a strong predictor of future achievement. The better readers we are early on, the stronger our capacity to achieve later on (Sparks, 2014). Helping pupils to love reading is one of the central tenets of and central to successful education (Ofsted, 2017).

Continued on next page

With the average reading age of an adult in the UK being nine years old, it is incumbent on schools to do as much as possible to help pupils to read at the level of their chronological reading age. It is also the skill which will have the most impact on the pupil, opening up significantly more of the curriculum and therefore increased numbers of opportunities for success.

Every school has (and if not, should have) a reading programme in place that assesses the pupils' ability to read. It should also have a set of books which are graded according to difficulty and available for the pupil to borrow and read. However, the devil is in the detail and schools continue to battle with effectively implementing such reading programmes against other curricular or financial priorities. But what is more important than a child's ability to read? A key issue is in the staffing of such programmes. Should they be applied and run by experts in the pupil support department (high quality delivery by a small number of staff to a small number of pupils) or by tutors or English teachers (possibly less expert delivery, by and to a larger group). As with any school support programme, it is essential this is monitored and tracked for impact by those leading it to ensure it is having the necessary impact.

STRATEGY 9.7: Three before me (or brain – book – buddy – boss)

An excellent activity that requires pupils to be independent from the outset and helps develop their independent study skills in a subtle but fun way.

Outcome

Pupils can work more independently.

Timing of the activity: Early on and during a lesson/topic

Every lesson in which pupils need to demonstrate better/more independent learning.

A useful strategy for also developing: knowledge and resilience.

Resources

Key points/grade descriptors displayed on the board. Seating arrangement: in fours

How it works

- Rule: Each pupil must speak to three other pupils before the teacher.
- A pupil needs to get the answer to any question they have, from themselves, from their book, from another pupil (Brain, Book, Buddy), or asking up to three pupils (Three), before asking the teacher (Me/the Boss).

Continued on next page

- This enables pupil questioning and peer feedback to be given before the teacher must intervene.

- A benefit of this strategy, especially with written work, is that a pupil also has three people checking their work before seeing the teacher. This helps reinforce the key points and measures of success being learnt and heightens the probability of pupils handing in a piece of work that is of a higher standard.

- The teacher checks the work afterwards.

- This approach also works well for pupils arriving late to a lesson or pupils who have attendance issues, as they can catch up with the work very quickly.

How will the teacher ensure learning has taken place?

Through displaying the rule and checking with the pupils that they have followed it before speaking to them.

How will progress be seen to be made?

Through pupils needing the help of the teacher less often.

STRATEGY 9.8: The invisible teacher

All the learning in this activity is led and done by the pupils. It helps them learn how to manage themselves and empathise with the role of being the teacher. This is an interesting, unique and high-risk activity in which the teacher takes no part until the end.

Outcome

By the end of the lesson, the pupils will have completed all the activities without the aid of the teacher, strengthening their problem-solving abilities and their ability to work independently.

Use of the strategy: later in a topic

Whenever pupils are ready, able and confident to take control of their learning.

A useful strategy for also developing: resilience and accuracy.

Resources

Role cards, instruction sheets, prizes.

Continued on next page

How it works

- The teacher prepares the room, organising instructions, information, role cards, prizes and the activities. They then sit on the side with a label on saying "Invisible Teacher".
- The pupils come into the lesson.
- The instructions as to what to do are on the board.
- Two pupils act as policemen to ensure that all instructions are carried out. They have the power to give merits and behaviour points as befits the behaviour of the class.
- There are a number of activities set and one must be completed first, followed by the others.
- Directions are found around the room.
- When all the tasks are done, the invisible box is opened and the prizes inside given to all the pupils that successfully completed all the tasks set.

How will the teacher ensure learning has taken place?

Through setting clear instructions and having the "policemen" check the pupils' work and award achievement points when the work is done.

How will progress be seen to be made?

Progress in this activity will be visible through pupils being more able to complete the tasks set on their own, without the help of the teacher.

ACTIVITY 9.9: Creative writing and speaking

This lesson is particularly good in helping pupils create and experiment with ideas in a safe environment, so that they have the confidence to do the work afterwards on their own.

Outcome

A short piece of creative writing or speaking. The pupils will have a clearer understanding of what is needed and how to create their narrative.

Timing of the activity: later in a topic

One lesson

A useful strategy for also developing: skills (writing, listening) and resilience.

Continued on next page

Resources

Keywords

How it works

- The teacher writes the title of the piece of work that needs to be created.

- In a circle, the class take it in turns to ask a question related to the theme and the next person answers it, developing the story further in terms of character, plot, dialogue and description.

- After two rounds, the teacher discusses with the class which questions drew out the best response and why, discussing the importance of adjectives, verbs and adverbs in storytelling.

- The class is then split into small groups and they continue to develop the plot and characters, the teacher insisting that pupils use good questions and more adjectives, verbs and adverbs.

- After two rounds, the teacher sees where each group has taken the story.

- The teacher splits the class into pairs and does the same again.

- Finally, everyone works on their own, finishing off the story in their own way.

- The pupils will now be ready and able to write their own piece of creative writing.

How will the teacher ensure learning has taken place?

The measure of success of this lesson is in the ability of the pupils to incrementally and consciously work independently.

How will progress be seen to be made?

Progress will be visible through pupils increasingly able to work on their own with no loss of quality to the story being created.

Implications for leaders: demonstrating impact inside the classroom

For the leader monitoring progress in independent learning in lessons, there are several tools available, these include observation, learning walks and homework analysis.

Quantitative measures: data analysis

Analysis of the data relating to homework/independent study being set and completed, or the change in reading ages of pupils through a reading programme is the clearest method of quantitively demonstrating impact in independent learning (EEF, 2019c). Progress over time should show all pupils being set and completing the expected amount of homework/independent study or for reading ages to increase.

Patterns in the data may emerge of individual pupils, small or large groups of pupils or teachers showing variations in that expectation. A question that would therefore arise for leaders is why are those patterns taking place? This may indicate that high expectations are unclear or impractical given certain subject areas. Either way issues that are indicated by the patterns in the data need to be addressed.

Qualitative measures: observations

Leaders wishing to see progress in independent learning in a lesson should be able to see this easily in an observation. During the lesson, the teacher should consciously change the dynamics and activities within the lesson, usually as the lesson progresses, so the pupils work increasingly independently.

Qualitative measures: learning walks

Learning walks may identify patterns across several classes and indicate the mindset to independent learning of a group of teachers. If there is a mindset of not structuring lessons to sufficiently accommodate independent learning or enabling pupils to more actively lead the learning in the lesson, then a learning walk around a faculty or the school will indicate whether there is a collective mindset for not enabling this as much as is needed.

As a result, learning walks are a good way of seeing how consistent the independent learning is within a faculty or group of classes.

Demonstrating impact outside the classroom

Homework

The school policy on homework should be up-to-date and fit for purpose. In my experience, schools do not monitor and track homework as rigorously as they could do. As a result, the quality of homework tends to decrease over the school year. Pupils only get one chance at being a pupil in, for example, Year 3, Year 6, or Year 10. It is essential if homework is to play an active and important role in pupil progress, that it is taken seriously be everyone and done well.

Progress in independent learning over time: programmes of study/ schemes of work/lessons

In the programmes of study, schemes of work or lessons, there should be clear progression with lessons being heavily teacher dependent at the start, to being more pupil independent at the end. Equally, it should be clearly mapped on the programme of study and scheme of work, how homework and independent study outside the classroom are being used to support the learning taking place inside the classroom.

Homework v interventions

For schools, there is an age-old conundrum, what to do when a pupil doesn't do their homework. Here are a couple of models and a short discussion on the merits of each.

Model 1: Don't set homework = Low maintenance/High follow-up/Low benefits

Not setting homework is incredibly high risk for schools and a risk not worth taking if a pupil's learning is at stake. However, if a school chose not to set homework, there would be little maintenance of the system (there isn't one) but would require much more follow-up in terms of classroom teaching and intervention should it be needed. As a result, there is little benefit to the pupils or the school in not setting homework.

Model 2: Homework is rigorously set = High maintenance/Low follow-up/High benefits

If homework is to be set, it is important, as mentioned earlier, to do the job properly and ensure it is set and completed well. Whilst this is a high maintenance system, requiring a leader to be monitoring and tracking a large number of interactions weekly, there should be increasingly minimal follow-up with staff or pupils increasingly doing what is expected of them, With high benefits for pupils and the school in the form of more work being completed as a result of the homework being done merits this model being followed.

Model 3: Prep = Low maintenance/Low follow-up/High benefits

The private sector has been doing this model for years and therefore are seasoned at it. Having a room full of pupils doing their homework, or prep, supervised by a few members of staff is a very efficient way of ensuring homework and independent study is completed. In this regard, there is little maintenance as the whole school essentially is on a staffed detention, whilst the pupils complete their homework.

As a result, there is also little follow-up as to who has or hasn't done their homework as all pupils will be there to do their homework. This appears to be the model that works best.

Model 4: Interventions after school = High maintenance/High follow-up/High benefits

One of the downsides of taking a relaxed approach with homework is that teachers can spend a large amount of time mopping up, spending time after school with pupils who are not making sufficient progress in class. This is highly inefficient. Teachers setting homework that may or may not be completed by pupils requires a large amount of follow-up on behalf of the school (leadership), thus being high maintenance. As a result, there is likely to be a large amount of follow-up due to the inconsistent nature of the setting and completion of the homework. However, it does ensure the work is done to the benefit of the pupil and the school.

Key questions

For teachers

1 How are you ensuring in your lessons that you are creating opportunities for and explicitly enabling pupils to be independent learners?

2 How are you ensuring in your lessons that you are explicitly teaching pupils to know how to successfully learn independently?

3 How are you making best use of homework and independent study to support the work in class?

4 How regularly are you consciously letting go and transferring to the pupils the ability to lead their own learning and learn without your input?

For leaders and governors

1 Are all staff clear about what independent learning is and how pupils demonstrate this in their lessons?

2 Do leaders and staff understand how to teach and enable pupils to be increasingly independent in their subject areas?

3 What does the monitoring and tracking of homework, independent study and any reading programmes tell you about how successfully pupils work independently?

4 How effective therefore is your homework policy? How do you know? Are other ways likely to be more effective?

5 How well do programmes of study and schemes of work specify and demonstrate increasing opportunities for independent learning?

6 What patterns emerge from the data and what does that tell you about how well pupils are working independently?

7 When you are observing lessons, how can you see progress being made in the pupils working independently?

8 When you are carrying out a learning walk of the school or a department, what evidence is there of pupils working with increasing independence in what they do?

For parents

1 What online facility does the school have for parents to check and know when homework is set?

2 What does the school recommend you can do as a parent to help with your child's homework?

3 What websites does the school recommend to support your child's independent study?

4 What opportunities are available with family, trusted friends and colleagues to help your child be increasingly confident as an independent learner and an independent young adult?

ENDNOTE

Progress in practice: lessons learnt in independent learning – their story

Setting homework is an easy win for teachers, until you have to mark it! It is also the opportunity to take everything you have taught them and take that to another level, to allow pupils the opportunity to fly.

One of my Music pupils for his GCSE composition homework decided he would compose a piece of serialism. In a nutshell, it's a piece where you have to use all twelve notes in an octave once before you can use them again. It's a lot like constructing musical Sudoku. He brought it in and marking it, it was perfect. Literally, not a note out of place. He went on to get his A*.

One of the joys of being a senior leader is that you get to teach subjects other than your specialism. Teaching English and getting to know the Gothic Horror genre was a particularly memorable project. Not only for the wonderful opportunities to teach but also for what it inspired. One of the pupils in the class for one of her homework's went away and came back next lesson with a small book. She had gone home, created and typed up her gothic horror story in the style of a book and then bound it. One of the best homework's I have had the pleasure to mark both in style and in content.

Similarly, in another class when working on script writing for television, a pair of pupils produced a pair of scripts for their homework. They were able to perform it to the class and everyone was hugely entertained by their writing and performance.

Finally, and this occurs rarely in education, one of the pupils achieved A*s in all their GCSE exams. Truly fantastic. When asked about what the secret was to their success was, the reply came back, "I just did everything my teachers told me to do".

My old singing teacher, when I was applying for universities said to me "Aim high. Let the universe decide the limit of your success, not you. You never know how far you can go". This has stayed with me and something I regularly use in assemblies and in class.

Setting homework and allowing pupils the opportunity to take everything you have taught them and fly is one of the great joys of education. We should never deny the pupils that opportunity. As teachers, we should let the universe decide the limit of the pupils' success. Not us.

We never know how far they will fly.

# Progress across
the school

10 Progress: implications for assessment

Progress in assessment plain and simple:

Progress in assessment is in being
able to demonstrate sufficient learning when
that learning is put to the test.

In this chapter, we will cover:

- What we mean by assessment
- Formative assessment
- Summative assessment
- Grading

Introduction

Having clarified what we mean by progress, explored what other writers have said about progress and unpacked what progress looks like over time and in the classroom, we now come to assessment; the markers, the milestones that help us identify how much progress has been made.

It is important from the outset to differentiate between two different types of assessment indicators: formative assessment – assessment *for* learning (How well are we doing? Answered through marking, feedback, self and peer assessment) and summative assessment – assessment *of* learning (How well have we done? Answered through assessments, tests, examinations). Both have different functions and therefore *where* they are utilised in the learning process is important and significant.

Formative assessment in the classroom: assessment for learning

The importance of sharing success criteria and feedback from the start

Formative assessment is used in the early stages of learning about a topic, helping the teacher and the pupil come to a clearer understanding of the skills and knowledge to be learnt and the standards to be expected by the end of the scheme of work. There are two essential pieces of the puzzle that need to be in place for this to be effective. Firstly, it is essential that the *assessment criteria* are shared with the pupils from the outset. In this way the pupils are clear, to use the walking metaphor, where the top of the mountain is, and whilst we may be still far off, we can see and understand the end point of our educational journey.

As learning is *sequential,* just like walking up a mountain, taking one step at a time, we can only learn one lesson at a time. Hence, the importance for teachers of *sequencing* the learning as coherently and clearly as possible. Assessing how well we have achieved those steps requires a set of specific, smaller criteria related to the overall journey, so that both the pupils and the teacher understand and can recognise how far along their learning journey they have progressed. Thus, the need for the success criteria to be shared and explicit from the beginning.

The second part of the jigsaw is *feedback*; how much and how well the pupils have learnt in relation to the success criteria. The teacher being the expert, it is necessary early in the process to give feedback to each of the pupils as to how well they are doing. This will help minimise the possibility for mistakes and misunderstandings to happen later by the pupil.

This also helps the teacher to model how feedback should be done. Progress will be able to be seen when pupils are able to peer-assess and self-assess and have an opportunity to explore, discuss and engage with the assessment criteria for themselves. As a result, pupils should be able to assess themselves more accurately and effectively, and therefore get more out of the assessment experience than would otherwise be the case.

On the way to summative assessment: indicators of progress

As the pupil makes their way along their educational journey, there will come key points to stop and see how far they have travelled, how much has been learnt. This is when teachers need to see indicators of progress, educational milestones. The following summarises the book's five core themes and presents their indicators of progress to help teachers and pupils recognise the progress being made.

Skill: Incremental improvements through: Increases in the difficulty and complexity of the work; increased mastery; higher order thinking and responses; the work completed is harder.

Indicators of progress in skills: How sufficiently more skilled a pupil is than they were at the start.

Knowledge: Incremental improvements through: Increases in understanding; pupils are more knowledgeable, more engaged. Pupil responses to questioning are more detailed and more complex.

Indicators of progress in knowledge: How sufficiently more knowledgeable a pupil is than they were at the start.

Accuracy: Incremental improvements through: Increased accuracy of language or action; able to do something more frequently right, less frequently wrong; re-drafted work is more accurate; work corrected shows an understanding of what it means to be accurate; work is neater.

Indicators of progress in accuracy: How sufficiently more accurate a pupil is than they were at the start.

Resilience: Incremental improvements through: Pupils being able to solve and overcome challenges in their work; more work completed in a set amount of time; the same amount of work completed in a shorter amount of time; pupils are able to show and demonstrate an increasing ability to problem solve on their own.

Indicators of progress in resilience: How sufficiently more resilient a pupil is than they were at the start.

Independence: Incremental improvements through: Pupils being able to learn more independently; less teacher input, more pupil input to the lesson; pupils can increasingly work on their own successfully.

Indicatotrs of progress in independent learning: How sufficiently more able to work independently a pupil is, than they were at the start.

Summative assessment in the classroom: assessment of learning

Summative assessments test the learning to date and therefore come at the end of an educational journey; at the end of a topic or project. Unlike formative assessment, the success criteria are not necessarily shared before a test and the work of the pupil is almost always assessed individually.

This emphasises the need for the teacher to build up their pupils' resilience muscles and help them to be increasingly confident and comfortable working on their own, sooner rather than later.

Tests and assessments

End-of topic tests and assessments are a great way of seeing how much pupils' have learnt over the course of a topic, but on their own, may paint an imprecise picture of how well a pupil would perform in an end of year assessment. To get a more realistic view of how much the pupils have learnt over the year, the teacher can set the test/assessment in two halves: section A testing the most recently learnt topic and then a section B testing previously learnt work.

In this way, the test/assessment will be more indicative and informative as to how well pupils have remembered previously taught work in comparison to the most recent work and vice versa. As a result, interleaving topics, mixing in previously taught topics to the revision and lesson schedule provide significant benefit for the pupils.

Exams

A further area for consideration with summative testing is the language of the testing. Getting pupils used to the language used in exams as early as possible helps pupils understand them sooner and therefore more able to understand, process and answer them, more able to respond in exam-style language.

Exam conditions

In a similar way to test questions being set in the language of exams, the taking of tests should be as close as possible to the experience pupils will have in the final exam. As such, the possibility should be explored of re-creating exam conditions, especially for core subjects for all summative tests.

Exams should have a set protocol which is always followed, so that pupils, at what is the most challenging and tense time of their lives, can practise experiencing the exams in a way that is as well supported as possible.

Grading: a word of warning

As Mark Twain once said, there are lies, damn lies and statistics. It is essential that any school is clear on their rationale and method of assessment and that all leaders and teachers understand how they work. Let me explain why.

At the end of a topic, teachers are usually asked to give two grades – an effort grade (how hard the pupil has worked over the topic) and an achievement grade (the standard of work achieved by the pupil at the end of topic).

So far so good.

Looking at the Figure 10.1, the assessment grid for Daniel in Year 8, the end of topic assessment grades are crystal clear. However, depending on the school's rationale as to how these topic grades are brought together to report a final overall grade for Daniel in English at this moment in time can give highly varying numbers.

Rationale 1: Latest grade achieved
Calculation: Latest Topic (Topic 5): grade = 5 + Latest Test: grade = 6 = 11 / 2 = 5.5
English grade for Daniel submitted by the teacher = 5

Rationale 2: Forecast grade
Calculation: Target grade = 8.
Latest topic grade = 5, three more topics to go; previous topics scored highly.
Latest assessment grade = 6. Three more topics to go. With effort, the forecast grade should be achieved.
English grade for Daniel submitted by the teacher = 8

Daniel	8A	English
TOPIC	TOPIC GRADE (1 – 9)	TEST GRADE (1 – 9)
Topic 1 (12.5%)	6	6
Topic 2 (12.5%)	7	6
Topic 3 (12.5%)	8	7
Topic 4 (12.5%)	7	7
Topic 5 (12.5%)	5	6
Topic 6 (12.5%)		
Topic 7 (12.5%)		
Topic 8 (12.5%)		
Target Grade	8	

Figure 10.1 Daniel's Assessment Report – Easter

Rationale 3: Average grade achieved to date

Calculation: Average topic grade (6.6) + Average test grade (6.4) = 13 / 2 = 6.5

English grade for Daniel submitted by the teacher = 6

Rationale 4: Average grade achieved to date, taking the whole year into account

Calculation: Average topic grade (33/8) = 4.125 + Average test grade (34/8) = 4.25 = 8.375 / 2 = 4.2

English grade for Daniel submitted by the teacher = 4

Which is accurate? Which is right?

As can be seen, four different assessment rationales produce four different report grades for Daniel.

Therefore, if the school doesn't get the assessment rationale right and consistent with all teachers and leaders, pupils can be seriously misrepresented in their school grades, not by their work, but by the mechanisms by which the school creates their data.

Key questions

For teachers

1 How are baseline assessments created? What do they mean?

2 What is the policy regarding assessment for pupils who are persistently absent or who have just arrived in the school?

3 What is the assessment schedule for the year?

4 What is the school's expectation of marking?

5 How does the school want me to report summative test grades and how often?

For leaders and governors

1 What is the school's rationale for assessment? How is this communicated and checked?

2 What is the school's expectation as to how grades are calculated and presented?

3 What is the school's position on outliers being taken into consideration when reporting data?

4 How often and how consistently are we assessing pupils?

5 How clear are we with staff, pupils and parents about assessment?

6 What are we expecting to see regarding formative and summative assessment?

7 Do all schemes of work and programmes of study make clear the assessment schedule for the year?

8 How are we quality assuring that all tests incorporate interleaving and the grade submitted is representative of the pupil's learning since the start of the year?

9 Are our expectations of marking and feedback clear? Are these consistent with all staff?

For parents

1 What is my child's baseline test score and target grade in each subject?

2 How often is my child going to be tested using internal and national or standardised testing?

3 What does this mean for me as a parent?

4 How often can I expect to see my child's work being marked?

5 How will the school keep me informed of my child's progress?

Progress: implications for leaders

In this chapter, we will cover leading progress in relation to:

- Vision and expectations
- Leadership and planning
- Information, advice and guidance
- Management and delivery
- Monitoring and tracking
- Support, CPD and interventions
- Evaluation and celebrating success

Introduction

In Section 1, we considered progress from the perspective of teachers and other writers and researchers in the field. In Section 2, we delved more deeply into what progress looks like in the classroom in terms of teaching, learning and assessment. We now turn to explore progress from the perspective of the school leader; the professionals responsible for ensuring that both the teachers and pupils complete their educational journeys successfully and on time. This chapter offers a bank of questions for school leaders to help focus, coupled with recommended actions to help deliver improved progress and contribute to whole school success.

Vision and expectations

Whether leading a group of schools, a single school or being part of the team that leads a school, the vision and the expectations from that vision are what drives the school and make it the success that it is. As a result, it is essential that progress is clearly embedded in the school's vision, ethos and language from the start.

Questions for leaders: A clear vision and set of expectations that deliver progress
In relation to supporting and ensuring pupils make and exceed the progress of which they are able:

➤ What is the school's vision and how clearly is progress encapsulated within it?

➤ What is expected of pupils/staff/leaders/parents in relation to this vision?

➤ How will they know this? How are these expectations being communicated?

➤ Where will these expectations of progress and targets be made explicit?

➤ How will pupils, staff and leaders understand what they need to do?

➤ How will pupils, staff and leaders understand how to do it?

➤ How will school leaders check this?

Encapsulating a vision: Five strap lines that have progress at the heart of what they do.

Achieving Excellence Together

Everyone Successful Everyday

The Harder I Work, The Smarter I Get

Together, Everyone Accomplishes More

We Enter to Learn, We Leave to Achieve

Recommendations for leaders

✓ All: On the school website, presentations, lesson PowerPoints and the school letterhead, the school's strapline, its vision and mission in a nutshell, should be stated for all to see.

✓ Leaders: Look at fifty similar schools and where their achievement is better, see what they are doing to make the difference.

✓ Pupils and staff: Set high expectations in everything a school does and never let them drop.

✓ Pupils and staff: Make sure pupil targets are in all exercise books, on all reports and on all lesson PowerPoints. Make sure all staff targets are included in line management notes and other relevant documents. No one should ever be unclear about what their targets are.

✓ Pupils and staff: Have a non-negotiables poster displayed in every classroom. It can communicate the vision and expectations succinctly to pupils and teachers regarding expectations and progress.

✓ Staff: Ensure the Code of Conduct, relevant policies and the Staff Handbook all make explicit the vision and expectations of staff regarding progress.

✓ Parents and the community: Ensure the prospectus, school newsletter and website communicate the vision and expectations, clearly and succinctly, to parents and the local community, in relation to progress and how they can contribute.

✓ Set out the expectations of responsibility, accountability and a no excuses culture from the start:

❖ If you teach a class: you're responsible;

❖ If you lead a department: you're responsible;

❖ If you have a specific responsibility: you're responsible;

❖ If you have a whole school responsibility: you're responsible.

✓ Whatever is done and however it is done, consistency in all is key.

Leadership and planning

So that the teaching and learning that needs to take place goes as smoothly and successfully as we would wish, school leaders need a plan. Any plan needs to be clear, comprehensive and coherent.

Questions for leaders: Clear leadership and planning that deliver progress

➤ What plans need to be in place, so everyone knows what they are doing and by when?

➤ Do all plans and other key documents have progress and targets front and centre within them?

➤ What are the measures of success so that the school knows how well they are doing?

➤ What level/standard/number needs to be reached to be successful?

➤ Similarly, what level/standard/number needs to be reached to be unsuccessful?

➤ What are the key milestones and key dates to check the school is on track to achieve its goal?

➤ Are all curriculum maps, programmes of study and schemes of work in place, up-to-date and fit for purpose?

Recommendations for leaders

✓ Have a school template for lesson presentations, curriculum maps, programmes of study and schemes of work to ensure consistency across the school.

✓ Ensure the development plans, line management minutes and other key documents have the key school targets front and centre.

✓ Have an overview of all deadlines, especially in exam groups, that can be managed, monitored and checked.

✓ Have a scheduled time set up each term to review and re-organise classes so pupils with similar needs are in the same class.

✓ Have a homework schedule in place for the year which supports the learning in lessons.

✓ Where appropriate/necessary/effective, allocate under-timetabled staff to support exam classes first, then underachieving subjects, with small group work/ team teaching.

✓ Allocate under-timetabled supply/cover teachers to support exam classes first, then underachieving subjects with small group work/team teaching.

✓ Provide a planned, co-ordinated mandatory intervention / support programme for key pupils/key groups. This should include a weekly plan/report card for underachieving pupils.

✓ On the timetable, set up a last period Intervention lesson, for underachieving pupils to attend.

✓ Set up an annual review and check of all curriculum maps, programmes of study and schemes of work to check they are up-to-date and fit for purpose?

✓ Set up an action group to secure progress for key groups and meet monthly to monitor progress.

Information, advice and guidance

Without the effective communication of clear information, advice and guidance, there is a risk that whatever vision and detailed plans we have in place as school leaders may come to naught. It is therefore essential that leaders consider the information that is needed to be communicated and the best method for that communication in relation to securing progress.

Questions for leaders: information, advice and guidance that deliver progress

➤ What information, advice or guidance is in place for pupils, staff, parents and governors about what the pupils are going to learn in the school?

➤ What information, advice or guidance is in place for pupils, staff, parents and governors about how well pupils are making progress in their learning at the school?

➤ What information, advice or guidance is in place for pupils, staff, parents and governors about assessments, tests, examinations and the preparation for them?

➤ How effectively are communication methods (e.g. PSHE lessons, assemblies and tutor time to pupils, meetings and bulletins to staff, the school website and newsletters to parents) being used to communicate key information, advice and guidance to support pupil progress?

Recommendations for leaders

✓ Ensure that a template to communicate expectations, curriculum guidance and tracking of progress to pupils, staff and parents is in place and consistent.

✓ Always model what you ask people to do.

✓ Have a "Year Ahead Evening" for each year group to outline the expectations and key information for parents, pupils and staff.

✓ Ensure the Staff Handbook is up-to-date, fit for purpose and includes clear classroom routines.

✓ Implement a whole-school lesson plan template to ensure consistency across the school.

✓ Have a rolling agenda item in key meetings to discuss and share classroom best practice.

✓ Where relevant, secure a budget and purchase in good time, revision guides for pupils.

✓ Where necessary, secure a budget and purchase in good time, textbooks for all subjects.

✓ Use an online shared area such as Google Drive to create a curriculum resources bank for staff.

✓ Use an online shared area, such as Google Drive or the school website, to create a curriculum information bank for pupils and parents.

✓ Use an online shared area, such as Google Drive or the school website, to provide pupils and parents with a list of useful websites, programmes of study and exam specifications.

✓ Ensure all policies are kept up-to-date and that what is practised is what it says in the policy.

✓ Review and ensure tutor time and PSHE lessons help pupils with their learning skills, knowledge, resilience and ability to work independently.

✓ Following any tests, pupils should Red Amber Green (RAG) rate their tests and compile a list of topics, so that they can prioritise their own follow-up revision. Where possible, these lists should be linked to (online) resources such as practice questions and the ability to self-test.

Management and delivery

So that the teaching and learning that needs to take place goes as smoothly and successfully as we would wish, and lessons go as planned, school leaders need to successfully manage the delivery of that plan; as a result, avoiding any frustration arising from a lack of time or resources to do what needs to be done in the time frame required.

Questions for leaders: effective management that delivers progress

➤ What staffing and resources need to be in place and by when so that pupils, staff, leaders and parents can do what they need to do to support the pupils with their learning?

➤ What budget is needed to (further) support progress and how is this to be sourced?

➤ How is the budget to be managed and controlled to ensure it doesn't go over-budget?

➤ Has enough time been allocated so that all teachers can teach the full curriculum in good time? How do you know this?

➤ What additional time (e.g. homework allocation/after school slots) can be utilised if needed?

➤ What safety nets of time, money or resources are in place should any difficulties arise?

Recommendations for leaders

✓ Prioritise your workload so that the important, complex, larger, urgent work is prioritised ahead of less important, less complex, smaller and less urgent work.

✓ Encourage staff to say "no" when leaders ask them to do anything that takes them away from teaching and learning.

✓ Similarly, be firm with yourself in saying "no" to outsiders who have wonderful unrelated ideas and offers that can seriously draw staff and pupils away from the core business of teaching and learning.

✓ Delegate work to your bosses (yes, to your bosses!) and to your team when necessary, so that you manage your own workload and ensure what needs to be done by you is successfully completed by the deadline.

✓ Develop staff potential into staffing reality. Identify the staff that are delivering consistently great teaching in the classroom and put them into positions of responsibility and influence. Help the school grow.

✓ Teach pupils how to study. Never assume they know how to do this.

✓ Consider setting up a study room/revision room for 3–4 nights a week after school up to 5pm, and during half-term break 9am–4pm, staffed by SLT/teachers on a voluntary basis. Food and drink may be provided as an incentive.

✓ Ensure homework is targeted and used as preparation for lessons or the practice and reinforcement of previous learning.

✓ Ensure homework and revision are always specific and relate to pages within textbooks and revision guides.

To ensure the work of the school is effectively managed when things don't go as well as they should, it's so important that leaders do what they need to do with the staff they lead. When done well, it puts staff back on the right track quickly and supportively. Should matters get worse, and the situation goes further (capability or disciplinary), the leader has done everything by the book. What follows is guidance I use with leaders which you may find useful.

Procedures for leaders to follow up issues with staff, once an issue has been identified....

Meeting 1 – concern

Middle leader sets up meeting between member of staff and themselves. Clarify issue.
   Identify success criteria/support and agree improvement. Confirm target(s) and a time frame.
   Follow up the meeting with an email with what was agreed and when to be reviewed (cc relevant SLT).

Meeting 2 – review concern

Middle leader sets up review meeting between member of staff and themselves.
   Clarify issue and what was agreed to improve.

Continued on next page

Review progress against success criteria/effectiveness of support and whether targets are met.

Follow up the meeting with an email (c.c.' to relevant SLT). If target/success criteria met – close (including an "However, should there be a recurrence…."). If not, hand on to SLT for Meeting 3.

Meeting 3 – serious concern

SLT sets up meeting between member of staff, middle leader and SLT

Clarify issue, including the failure to address issue previously.

Identify new success criteria/support and agree improvement plan. Confirm target(s) and a time frame.

Follow up the meeting with an email as to what was agreed and when to be reviewed (cc HT).

Meeting 4 – review serious concern

SLT sets up review meeting between member of staff, middle leader and SLT.

Clarify issue and what was agreed as the improvement plan.

Review progress against success criteria/effectiveness of support and whether targets met.

Follow up the meeting with a letter (ccd to HT). If target/success criteria met – close (including an "However, should there be a recurrence…."). If not, hand on to HT.

Meeting 5 – continued serious concern

HT sets up meeting between member of staff, union rep (if needed), SLT and HT.

Clarify issue, including continued failure to address issue, confirming if this to be addressed through capability or disciplinary procedures.

Identify new success criteria/support and agree improvement plan. Confirm target(s) and a time frame.

Follow up the meeting with a letter as to what was agreed and when to be reviewed.

Meeting 6 – review continued serious concern

HT sets up review meeting between member of staff, union rep, SLT and HT.

Clarify issue and what was agreed as the improvement plan.

Review progress against success criteria/effectiveness of support and whether targets met.

Follow up the meeting with a letter. If target/success criteria met – close (including an "However, should there be a recurrence…."). If not, follow up with formal capability or disciplinary procedures.

Monitoring and tracking

So that the teaching and learning goes as smoothly and successfully as we would wish, things go as planned and we cover everything that needs to be covered on time, leaders need to ensure the plan is monitored and tracked to make progress and success a certainty, not a wishful hope.

Questions for leaders: monitoring and tracking that delivers progress

➣ In what way are you going to monitor, track and report on progress – with pupils, staff, parents and governors?

➣ What are your measures of success to secure strong progress in relation to pupil skills, knowledge, accuracy, resilience and independence?

➣ What level/standard/number needs to be reached to be successful?

➣ Similarly, what level/standard/number needs to be reached to be unsuccessful?

➣ In what way are you going to celebrate success where enough progress is made with pupils, staff and leaders?

➣ In what way are you going to follow up informally and formally where insufficient progress is made with pupils, staff and leaders?

Recommendations for leaders

✓ If not already done, book onto an Excel spreadsheet course, or get the school to set up an Excel workshop for leaders. The sooner they are well versed in using spreadsheets, the better.

✓ Use RAG-ed question/skills analysis to monitor classes/groups and focus on urgently improving Red (poorly learnt) topics.

✓ Consider having two exercise books per child – an exercise book for rough work and an assessment book for final, finished or assessed work.

✓ Make sure pupils are given time to respond to and improve their RAG-ed work.

✓ Administer rigorous follow-up of deadlines. See pupils, staff and leaders who do not meet deadlines and resolve any issues. See procedures for leaders.

✓ Use data analysis. Analysis of the assessment data is the clearest method of demonstrating impact. Progress over time should show all pupils achieving at or above the expected level of attainment, that's the aim.

2

2

2

✓ Use book looks: Looking through pupils' books, there should be clear progress in the increasing difficulty of the work from the start of the book to the most current work. For example, through:

❖ Tracking sheets – completed tracking sheets in pupils' books show the pupils attaining higher grades as they are more able to demonstrate more difficult work over time.

❖ More complex language – The language being learnt and written is increasingly more complex through the book. More keywords are more accurately used and indicate progress in understanding and expression of the skills being learnt.

❖ More complex writing – The complexity of the writing with more compound and complex sentences, increased use of adjectives and adverbs, as pupils think more clearly and skilfully are indicators of progress in writing skills.

❖ More technical feedback – The feedback given to the pupils, through self-assessment, peer assessment or teacher assessment, and the responses to that feedback, is increasingly technical, showing a higher degree of understanding of the skills being understood.

✓ Use observations: Observations of lessons will be able to indicate how effectively the lesson is being taught by the teacher and learnt by the pupils. During the lesson, the teacher should be teaching, and the pupil should be learning increasingly difficult skills and knowledge, more accurately and more independently as both the lesson and especially the year progresses.

✓ Use learning walks: Learning walks will identify patterns across several classes and indicate the mindset of a group of teachers. A learning walk around a faculty or the school will indicate whether there are collective strengths that need recognising and celebrating; the level of implementation of new initiatives, or collective issues that need addressing.

Support, CPD and interventions

The business of a school is education; for all its pupils by all its staff. As such, there will be many times when pupils, staff, leaders, governors and parents don't know, or are unable to do something as well as they might. This is especially true when securing progress for target key groups, including boys, girls, Special Educational Needs (SEN) pupils, disadvantaged pupils and pupils whose first language isn't English. To minimise the possibly high levels of anxiety in such situations, it is necessary for leaders to ensure the most effective support, training and interventions are delivered to teachers and leaders in a supportive, positive, constructive and timely way.

Questions for leaders: clear support and training that deliver pupil progress

➤ What key skills are needed by pupils, staff, leaders and parents to help pupils progress?

➤ How will you check and then know they have the skills they need to secure pupil progress?

➤ What will you do to support/train them if they don't have the skills they need?

➤ What specific support and guidance will you provide to support your target groups?

Recommendations for leaders

For pupils, staff and parents:

✓ Arrange specific assemblies and meetings to communicate exam preparation expectations and support.

✓ Consider booking an effective motivational speaker to help focus pupils, staff and parents on learning and exam preparation.

✓ Put schemes of work, recommended revision guides and useful revision websites on the school website for parents and pupils to access.

For staff:

✓ Have a fortnightly meeting with middle and senior leaders to ensure consistency of teaching and learning across the school.

✓ Agree amongst staff what a year's progress looks like (Hattie, 2015).

✓ Buddy up weaker staff with stronger staff until they are consistently better.

✓ Empower staff and leaders to review themselves against a set of standards (Teachers' Standards, Leaders' Standards).

✓ Use Performance Appraisal as a centralised CPD audit for teachers and leaders.

✓ Ensure teachers are expert in diagnosis, interventions and evaluation in what they do.

✓ Use your best teachers and leaders to support and coach weaker teachers and leaders.

✓ Strengthen and empower teachers through using every CPD opportunity to celebrate expertise and embed good teaching practice.

For pupils:

✓ If in a mixed school, consider single sex lessons or after school interventions.

✓ Use after school time to support target groups, especially for additional intensive study.

✓ On the timetable, set up a last period intervention lesson, for underachieving pupils to attend.

✓ All staff to mentor an underachieving pupil and guide successfully through with a weekly report and completion of weekly targets.

✓ Provide a voluntary working lunch: Lunchtime sessions with pupils and teacher as prep or follow-up.

✓ Exam preparation – Review work in class – revise work for homework – test in hall – an exam paper at least every fortnight leading up to exams.

✓ Independent learning – Allow independent revision time for the best pupils as an incentive for the others.

✓ In tutor times or lessons, draft in Sixth Form mentors to support individual pupils with completion of their (course) work or reading practice.

✓ For pupils one grade away from their target grade, work in small groups (4–6 per class). Identify common weak topics. Set targeted homework, with specific revision tasks and after school intervention sessions scheduled and centrally coordinated.

Evaluation and celebrating success

As a leader, all the work that goes into our life at school needs to be recognised and celebrated. It is equally as important to be able to bring together summative information in a clear, comprehensive and coherent way, identifying areas for improvement as well as the hard and successful work completed by the school community, which requires both recognition and celebration.

Questions for leaders: clear evaluation that values pupil progress and celebrates success.

➤ What quantitative methods (e.g. closed question questionnaires or test results) are you going to use to evaluate progress in your area? What is the measure of success?

➤ What qualitative methods (e.g. open question questionnaires or feedback) are you going to use to evaluate progress in your area? What is the measure of success?

➢ How are you going to evaluate and judge the effectiveness of the interventions you use?

➢ What are the reasons behind the successes in progress?

➢ What are the reasons behind the lack of success in progress?

➢ What are you going to do differently and better in future as a result?

➢ How will you report your findings to pupils/staff/leaders/governors/parents?

➢ Most importantly, how are you going to celebrate their successes?

Recommendations for leaders

✓ Evaluation: Carry out an annual Internal Quality Assurance Review on any under-achieving departments and a bi-annual audit on all other departments. Alongside the heads of department, this should include data analysis, lesson observations, learning walks, interviews with leaders, teachers and pupils, a work scrutiny of books and folders and any other documentary evidence.

✓ Evaluation: Carry out an annual External Quality Assurance Review on any repeatedly under-achieving departments and a bi-annual review across the whole school. Alongside the senior leadership team with a qualified school inspector, the review should include data analysis, lesson observations, learning walks, interviews with leaders, teachers and pupils, a work scrutiny of books and folders and any other documentary evidence.

✓ Evaluation: Wherever possible, encourage staff and leaders to be moderators, markers and assessors for their subject areas, upskilling them and able to share best practice with others.

✓ Celebration: Use your wall space! Celebrate your best pupils' achievements with individual posters celebrating their achievement with a photograph, their name, grade and destination.

✓ Celebration: Use your wall space! Celebrate your best pupils' achievements with a destination map showing the universities or employment pupils have gone to around the UK (or the world).

✓ Celebration: Use your wall space! Each faculty to celebrate their best pupils' achievements with posters celebrating a roll of honour for the best pupils in their subject in each year group.

✓ Celebration: Display the best completed pupil work that has been marked and annotated each half term.

✓ Celebration: In the weekly assembly, present a small prize to the Pupil of the Week for being nominated the most improved pupil that week.

12 Progress: implications for school evaluation

Progress in Evaluation plain and simple:

Progress in evaluation is a school being able to demonstrate clearly and simply how effectively the education provided is in securing progress for its pupils.

In this chapter, we will cover:

- ▉ Internal evaluation: Progress and the role of school leaders
- ▉ Internal evaluation: Progress and the role of governors
- ▉ External evaluation: Progress and the role of external support
- ▉ External evaluation: Progress and the role of school inspection
- ▉ Questions to help further understand and improve evaluations

Introduction

School evaluation is a big job.

It is harnessing thousands of lessons' worth of information and bringing it all together to form a judgement to answer a simple question: How effectively are the pupils in this school learning?

Having considered progress from the perspective of teachers, other writers and school leaders, from the perspective of teaching, learning and assessment, it is time for all the pieces that have been apart to come together. This chapter looks in more detail at what school leaders and governors need to do and be aware of in their evaluation of the work of the school in relation to progress and progress over time, so that their answer to the question "How effectively are the pupils in this school learning?" is a clear, simple and unequivocal one.

Internal evaluation: school leaders

Systems

Having effective systems in place is essential for any school to run teaching and learning consistently well. It is just as essential that school leaders understand how each system supports and helps improve pupil progress and that the measure of success for that system is clear and measurable. Examples of such systems include assessment, behaviour, homework and staff development.

Monitoring and tracking

So that leaders can be confident the school systems are working as effectively as they could be, it's also essential that what we do is monitored and tracked against our measures of success. This will help leaders identify areas of best practice that can be celebrated, modelled and disseminated to others as well as identify where work is less effective and requires further attention.

> Ensuring all classroom observations, learning walks and book scrutinies are done jointly with other leaders will help everyone be comfortable with working jointly with others, whether they be school leaders, governors, school improvement partners or school inspectors. This will also help keep leaders informed of current practice as well as embed consistency, provide useful leadership CPD and help validate/quality assure the evaluations made.

Evidence

This is the key area by which school leaders stand or fall. There are several areas for which school leaders need to ensure evidence is in place, up-to-date, regularly reviewed and evaluated.

The school website is the online front door to the school. As such, it holds an eminent position as the intermediary, first port of call for visitors and is the online representative for the school. Whilst we are counselled not to judge a book by its cover, first impressions count. Ensuring a school website has all the latest up-to-date information, policies and procedures on it is a key school priority.

Especially at the at the start of the school year or at the start of a half term, lessons are likely to be at the very beginning of a scheme of work and therefore lesson observations, learning walks or book scrutinies are likely to have little evidence of progress in skills development or knowledge acquisition in that topic. What matters here is that pupils have their targets in their books and are clear about where they are going with their learning. In addition, what school leaders/visitors see happening in lessons should be what it says in the scheme of work and programme of study.

> Essential for school leaders to clearly demonstrate how effective their school is, is in the evidence they can gather. Ensuring there is documentary evidence in place showing regular data analyses, lesson observations, learning walks, interviews with leaders, teachers and pupils and work scrutinies of books and folders is a basic requisite for any leader. NB – don't miss the obvious! What impact has attendance on progress? How do boys and girls differ with their progress? How have the SEN pupils and in-year admissions done? Having a brief analysis and short-term plan of action in place for anything that requires further attention and action is also vital.

Other key pieces of evidence to support the evaluations in teaching and learning are the tracking sheets, feedback, response to that feedback and the progress of the work in books. Regularly talking to pupils about their work, what they are aiming to achieve and learn and the progress they are making to achieve it also helps school leaders gauge the level of understanding of the pupils in their learning.

Further, using questionnaires and audits to evaluate the qualitative, softer aspects of school life, provides the harder evidence that can stand up to scrutiny should it be needed. This would include having regular staff, parent and pupil questionnaires and audits to evaluate the quality of learning and progress being made.

Finally, as mentioned earlier, with the average reading age of all adults in the UK being that of a nine-year old, it is essential that a whole school reading programme is in operation and that that the programme is being implemented, monitored and evaluated.

This all feeds into one of the most important documents in a school which is the school's self-evaluation of itself; the School Evaluation Form, or SEF.

This document assesses and evidences the school's current strengths and weaknesses in relation to the curriculum, teaching and learning, achievement, personal development and behaviour. A summary of the school's self-evaluation is the ultimate piece of evidence that helps the school evidence the answer to the question "How effectively are the pupils in this school learning?"

Recommendations for school leaders

✓ Systems: Ensure there are clear flow charts, processes or procedures in place, especially in relation to skills and knowledge acquisition.

✓ Ensure there is a ban on excuses. Everyone takes responsibility for their work, their progress and their achievement.

✓ Systems: Have clear measures of success with a lower baseline below which is a cause for concern, and above which is a cause for celebration and dissemination.

✓ Monitoring and tracking: Have all questionnaires and audits in place and consistent.

✓ Monitoring and tracking: Ensure all classroom observations, learning walks and book scrutinies are done jointly with other leaders. This will help embed consistency, provide useful leadership CPD and help validate/quality assure the evaluations made.

✓ Monitoring and tracking: Ensure monitoring and tracking spreadsheets are kept up-to-date and regularly (at least every half term) and evaluated with others.

✓ Evidence: Have up-to-date schemes of work and programmes of study in place and that lesson observations and learning walks evidence that these are all on track.

✓ Evidence: Ensure documentary evidence is in place of regular data analyses, lesson observations, learning walks, interviews with leaders, teachers and pupils, and work scrutinies of books and folders.

✓ Evidence: Have a whole school reading programme in operation (Drop Everything And Read – DEAR time) that is implemented and clearly monitored and evaluated.

✓ Evidence: Have a summary of the whole school self-evaluation in place and updated regularly.

Internal evaluation: governors

The role of the governor and the governing body in a school is that of Critical Friend. A group that holds ultimate responsibility and accountability for the school and, as such, needs to ensure that the school is being run as well as it possibly can be.

Criticality is experienced through the governors regularly holding to account the headteacher and the senior leaders running the school for their decisions and their work. In addition, the governors usually have a vested interest in the school (parent governors being the obvious example) and will be supportive champions of and for the school.

Their primary role is to ensure the school has a clear strategic direction so that the operational side of running a school (residing with the headteacher) is effectively delivered, so that the strategic goals are reached. As such, it is incumbent on the governing body to work with the headteacher to ensure there is a realistic long-term school improvement plan and a deliverable short-term school development plan in place.

Issues may arise here if Chairs of Governors, headteachers and/or key governors are relatively new to the role and therefore do not have the experience of an effective, deliverable strategic or school development plan. Having external advisors available to provide external expertise, guidance and external validation for such important planning is wise.

> The SEF is the receptacle for school self-evaluation. That said, they are rarely read. As such, they can (and should) be as short as possible. In response to the SEF, the School Development Plan (SDP) should also be as short but also inextricably linked to the SEF.

In ensuring the school has effective leadership, there is a need for governors to triangulate the information and evaluations presented to them through checking it out first-hand. Having a schedule of regular governor visits, inviting governors to key events such as parents' evenings, performances or results days, or linking governors to key areas of the school, for example, safeguarding, ensures the governing body has a comprehensive, collective understanding of how the school works and verifies the reporting and evaluations that are presented to them.

Another key role of governors is ensuring the school effectively carries out its statutory duties, essentially checking the checkers. This is a good way for governors to be clear about the statutory responsibilities of a school and ensuring those responsibilities are successfully carried out.

Having a regular slot at governors' meetings and on the school website for governors to share their experiences and keep the governing body and parents up-to-date will do much to ensure the governors effectively fulfil their role as critical friends.

Recommendations for governors

✓ Evidence: Have a 3–5-year school improvement plan and a one-year school development plan in place and updated regularly.

✓ Evidence: Have a governors training programme in place for the year, especially in how to read data and understand school acronyms and language.

✓ Evidence: Set up governors committees that are minuted and tie specifically to the key development areas of the school.

✓ Evaluation: Where a new Chair of Governors or a new headteacher is in role, utilise Local Education Authority (LEA) or local Teaching School Alliance expertise to provide external validation to plans and evaluations, especially at the start.

✓ Evaluation: Have a schedule of regular governor visits, having a "Governor of the Month", or invite governors to key events such as parents' evenings, performances or results days.

✓ Evaluation: Delegate key responsibilities to different governors (for example checking the Single Central Record is up-to-date) to regularly feedback to the rest of the governing body on progress.

External evaluation: LEAs and school improvement partners

The role of the LEA, Multi-Academy Trust (MAT) or School Improvement Partner (you've guessed it – SIP) is very different to the role of the governors, being a far more supportive role, providing external validation of the school's work as well as providing mentoring, coaching and feedback. For example, this could include supporting more effective teaching and learning, behaviour management or safeguarding. In brief, these agencies are usually working with a school to address a specific issue and, as such, will be there to provide both high challenge and high support to the school.

For this to be effective in relation to progress being made in the classroom, three pre-conditions need to be in place:

- *Clear Outcomes*: Clear agreement and understanding as to what is to be achieved in the set time frame.

- *Measurable Impact*: Clear agreement and understanding as to how success is to be measured and what the key milestones will be to signify enough progress is being made through the time of support.

- *A Formal Agreement*: Clear agreement and understanding of how the relationship, the roles and responsibilities will work between the school and the LEA, MAT or SIP needs to be in place. An agreement will also stipulate how the work is to be completed and reported.

As any reports from external evaluators can be used as evidence of school evaluation, it is essential that these reports are kept safe and available. Equally, as LEAs, MATs or SIPs can provide access to relatively affordable local expertise, for senior leaders to meet them regularly and develop a strong, supportive relationship would also be a wise move.

External evaluation: making school inspection as easy as possible

It is the call that every headteacher dreads.

It is the experience for every member of staff that is the most intense experience of their professional lives.

It is the school inspection.

The school inspection is necessary in providing a (arguably) consistent method by which the government can evaluate the quality of education across the country. Setting standards that define what effective education is, what effective leadership, governance, teaching and learning are, both informs and can stranglehold schools in meeting those standards.

Again, there are far more detailed books and internet articles that cover this area in more detail and discussing the pros and cons of school inspections here and now could seriously deviate us away from our theme. I will keep to three main areas related to school inspections: the work, the people and the environment.

The work

This is the central focus for a school inspection – how well does the school educate its pupils? What work are pupils doing? Is it sufficiently paced and challenging? What are the staff doing? Is what they are doing sufficiently enabling enough progress to be a real experience for the pupils?

The immediate place to start is inspecting the assessment data. This is the fruit of the school's work and will highlight areas where learning is going well and areas where it isn't. Patterns and themes are then picked up through scrutinising and inspecting pupils' books and files. Are they sufficiently full of work, kept to the best standard and show the best quality of learning?

Finally, the learning experience itself; inspecting lessons. Looking at the quality of learning taking place in lessons, whilst this is the end of the working trail for an inspection, it is the root of all teaching and learning and as such is the starting point to make the difference in progress.

The people

In observation, discussion and through responses to questionnaires, inspectors gain a view as to how effectively the school is working.

Discussions with pupils will illumine how embedded their learning is and how cogently and fluently they can talk about their learning. Observations of a significant sample of teachers teaching in the classroom will provide the evidence to determine the quality and consistency of teaching and learning across the school. Discussions with school leaders will help ascertain the strength and quality of leadership in the school and help triangulate the discussions with pupils and observations of staff. Finally, conversations with governors and reading the responses from parents and staff to questionnaires will add further confirmatory views to those already ascertained.

The environment

The first space any visitor to a school will see, including inspectors, is the reception area. As well as the school website (the online version of the school's reception area), the reception area is the biggest opportunity for a school to present and promote who it is, and how successful it is, as a school.

A subliminal message as visitors and inspectors walk around the school is given by the public spaces around the school regarding litter, displays and upkeep. Using the walls to paint inspirational messages and displays to celebrate success and promote progress are all low-cost opportunities to reinforce the message that our business as a school is about providing the best possible learning for our pupils.

Similarly, the classroom is the crucible of learning for the pupil. This environment should be a stimulating and enriching one, helping pupils to visually absorb a wealth of information.

External evaluation: school inspection today

In relation to the themes and messages outlined in this book and the current Ofsted inspection framework (Ofsted 2019b), there is much alignment. Below is a brief summary of the key themes outlined in Progress Plain and Simple and what the inspection framework requires of schools.

Intent: programmes of study and schemes of work

✓ There is clear consistency between school leaders regarding the knowledge and skills pupils need to learn.

✓ Both schemes of work and programmes of study have clear knowledge and skills as final outcomes.

✓ Consideration is made when designing schemes of work to be accessible to all pupils and that content is readable and age appropriate.

✓ Opportunities are built in for teachers to check and ascertain skills and knowledge gaps that pupils may have and are able to adjust the scheme of work or programme of study accordingly.

✓ Curriculum maps, schemes of work and programmes of study ensure the curriculum is clear, comprehensive and coherent and as a result new knowledge or skills are incorporated logically and smoothly.

✓ The curriculum offered to all pupils is in line with the National Curriculum, is broad, has a strong academic core and responsive to what the pupils need.

✓ An assessment programme evaluates pupils' knowledge and skills at the end of each scheme of work and each programme of study.

Intent: skills and knowledge

✓ Schools are ensuring they are teaching sufficient knowledge and cultural capital to pupils for them to succeed in life.

Implementation: knowledge, resilience, independence

✓ Knowledge: Teachers are expert (or supported to be expert) in what they teach.

✓ Knowledge: Teachers can help pupils understand and embed key concepts and complex theories.

✓ Knowledge: Knowledge is taught, and assessment is used to help pupils use knowledge fluently and deepen their understanding of the subject.

✓ Knowledge: There is a seamless link between old knowledge, new knowledge and that knowledge being applied through skills.

✓ Knowledge: Assessment assesses both short- and long-term learning.

✓ Resilience: Teachers check that pupils have learnt effectively and identify and correct any misunderstandings.

✓ Independence: Teachers ensure that pupils apply key concepts and complex theories fluently.

Impact: skills, knowledge, accuracy, resilience and independence

✓ Evidence will be gathered that show the pupils know more, can do more and remember more.

✓ Interviews and discussions with staff, leaders and pupils, work scrutinies and documentary evidence will all play the part as evidence of impact.

Personal development: skills, knowledge, accuracy and resilience

✓ Skills: Pupils can demonstrate social skills in different settings, including volunteering, cooperating with others and able to resolve conflicts effectively.

✓ Skills: Pupils can demonstrate skills and attitudes that enable them to participate fully and contribute positively to their school, community and life in modern Britain.

✓ Accuracy: Pupils can demonstrate that they understand the difference between right and wrong, can apply rules and laws to their own lives and therefore respect the laws of England.

✓ Resilience: Schools can teach pupils resilience and independence, but it may not always be as easy for pupils to then apply that immediately to their own experience.

✓ Resilience: Schools help develop pupils' confidence, resilience and knowledge so that they can keep themselves mentally healthy.

Recommendations for schools in preparation for inspections

✓ Have an "Ofsted Ready" inspection action plan in place. This should be checked each half term and include what documents and evidence the headteacher, school leaders, teachers, governors and pupils need to have up-to-date and to hand.

✓ Be clear about the latest framework, how it differs from previous inspections (for example curriculum intent) and ensure all governors and staff are aware of the updated changes.

✓ Have a termly pupil, staff and parent questionnaire to help identify strengths and areas of concern which should be addressed swiftly.

✓ Ensure the school's reception area is as welcoming as possible and presents the school's identity and successes clearly.

✓ Ensure classroom displays provide and reinforce for pupils the knowledge they need to know.

✓ Ensure displays in common areas celebrate success and promote progress in learning.

13 Concluding thoughts

So here we are at the end of this book.

I hope after reading it, you are a lot clearer and more informed about progress in the classroom.

If you are a teacher or school leader, I also hope it has given you more ideas to apply to lessons and increase the potential for progress being made with the teachers and pupils you know. As a result of reading this book, I hope these extra ideas will help to make ordinary interactions in lessons more extraordinary.

I believe the interaction between the teacher and the pupil in the classroom is *the* single thing, above all else, for schools to get right. If this improves and students make progress as a result, everything else follows. But classrooms aren't like that, schools aren't like that and the world isn't like that.

I want to change that. Hence this book.

My ambitious goal is to help every teacher be a better teacher, so that in return, the students they teach make more progress and are more successful as a result. I want teachers, parents, pupils, school leaders and governors to have a more informed language around progress and, as a result, have more meaningful conversations about progress.

If you are a teacher or a school leader, use this book to make a positive difference in your everyday practice.

If you are a parent, or a governor, use this book to inform your discussions and conversations with your school.

If you know someone who you think could use this book – recommend it to them. Help me achieve my goal in getting the best possible education for all the young people in our care.

In the spirit of this book, I would love to hear your feedback about the book. You can contact me at michael@schoolleaderdevelopment.com.

I look forward to hearing from you.

All my best wishes,

Mike

14 Suggested books and websites

Useful websites

Below are several suggested websites that provide further useful information and reference for teachers, leaders, parents and pupils, especially with regard to skills and knowledge development.

Websites

All subjects	https://www.bbc.co.uk/bitesize/ **BBC bitesize** is a great site for both KS3 and KS4 pupils in most subject areas. A really useful site for homework, independent study or revision.
	https://www.tes.com/teaching-resources **TES teaching resources** have over 700 000 resources for teachers in all subject areas. Log in and search away.
	https://www.khanacademy.org/ For pupils, parents or teachers, **Khan Academy** offers practice exercises, instructional videos, and a personalized learning dashboard that empower learners to study at their own pace in and outside of the classroom.
	https://quizlet.com/en-gb **Quizlet** enable teachers and pupils to use pre-made quizzes or set up their own, to help test the knowledge learnt so far.
	Wordwall.net **Word wall** has excellent resources for pupils to revise from and is an easy way for teachers to create their own teaching resources - quizzes, match ups, word games, and much more.
	https://www.teachingideas.co.uk/subjects/ **Teaching Ideas** is a fun, interactive website with lots of fun ideas for teachers to create lessons across a number of subjects.

	https://www.educake.co.uk/ **Educake** is a Maths, English, Science and Geography study site. Low stakes testing for pupils; quick understanding of problem areas for teachers.
	https://getrevising.co.uk/ resources?q=&level_id%5B%5D=gcse&level_id%5B%5D=standard_grade&l **Get revising** is a study room mainly for GCSE and A Level pupils to log on and revise.
Art	https://www.pinterest.co.uk/ **Pinterest** is designed for pupils and teachers to search and discover information through the format of images from the web. Many other users have created and shared 'pinboards' around many creative topics, themes and techniques.
	https://www.artsthread.com/ For pupils and teachers, **Artsthread** is primarily a website where aspiring artists and designers can upload and create an online profile. It connects creators to the industry by advertising competitions but also allows other young creatives to view each other's projects.
	https://frieze.com/ For teachers and pupils, **Frieze** is a website which collates creative industries through news, video, article and image. It describes itself as the definitive resource for contemporary art and culture.
	https://www.tate.org.uk/ The website connected to the gallery chain, **Tate** has upcoming exhibitions to see but also has many leaning and definition pages about art history and contemporary art with links to themes and artists pages. Useful for teachers, pupils and parents!
Dance	http://www.aqa.org.uk/subjects/dance/gcse/dance-8236 **AQA exam board** Useful Revision and assessment resources. https://www.amazon.co.uk/AQA-GCSE-Dance-Pupils-Book/dp/1408504197 **The AQA GCSE Dance pupil book** has a real focus on tracking individual progress, you can improve your pupils' chance of exam success through a unique blend of print and online resources.
Design & Technology	technologypupil.com **Technologypupil.com** provides a wealth of easy to navigate design and technology information sheets for pupils.
	mr-dt.com **Mr DT** provides 'quiz time' questions where pupils can test their design and technology material knowledge. Useful for teachers and pupils.
	http://wiki.dtonline.org/index.php/Main_Page **DT Online** is a resource for teachers and is a useful reference source to support design and technology study.
	design-technology.org Another site for teachers, **Design Technology.org** hosts a broad range of design and technology materials under clear, easy-to-navigate headings.

Drama	https://dramaresource.com/ **Drama Resource** is a website for teachers with lots of resources by David Farmer. Mainly aimed at the primary sector.
	https://www.dramatoolkit.co.uk/ **Drama Toolkit** is a resource and support website for Drama teachers, workshop facilitators and Drama practitioners. A one stop shop for all things Drama.
	https://www.londontheatre.co.uk/tickets/all-shows **London Theatre** website lists *every* performance taking place currently in London. (Theatre, dance, opera, comedy, etc.).
	https://www.shakespearesglobe.com/ **Shakespeare's Globe** is *the* place to visit for as close to an authentic Shakespearean theatrical experience as you will get anywhere.
English Language	https://www.cambridgeenglish.org/teaching-english/resources-for-teachers/ general-english-resources/ Website run by **Cambridge Assessment** – has a wealth of resources and information for pupils and teachers.
	https://www.teachingenglish.org.uk/resources/secondary **Teaching English** is a more international take for teachers on teaching English and practical resources for the classroom from the British Council
	http://www.onestopenglish.com/ With over 9000 resources, including lesson plans, worksheets, audio, video and flashcards, **onestopenglish** is the world's number one resource site for English Language.
English Literature	https://www.sparknotes.com/ **Spark Notes** offers support for teachers and pupils with Shakespeare, literature study guides and much more.
	https://www.litcharts.com/ Visiting **Lit Charts**, teachers can save time and stress with a host of support and information to download from this useful site.
	https://www.cliffsnotes.com/ **Cliff Notes** provides literature notes, test preparation and study guides for teachers and pupils.
Geography	https://www.cia.gov/library/publications/the-world-factbook/ **CIA** is a great site for both KS3 and KS4 pupils. You can use this site to compare countries and find the most up-to-date statistics.
	http://www.coolgeography.co.uk/ **Cool Geography** is a great site for KS4 pupils. You can use this to revise your case studies and examples.

	https://www.thoughtco.com/geography-4133035 **Thought Co**. is a great site for KS3 pupils. You can use this site for research projects.
	https://www.gapminder.org **Gap minder** is a great site for KS3 and KS4 pupils. Particularly useful when learning about global development and see some great examples of how data can be presented in geography.
History	https://spartacus-educational.com/ **Spartacus** is an excellent site for teachers wanting to go beyond the classroom, or for pupils or parents wanting to learn about a new area of history.
	https://www.history.co.uk **The History Channel** presents history in an accessible format and brings many areas to life in ways that are engaging and interesting. This is a great tool for pupils to build historical knowledge across a range of topics.
	https://www.history.org.uk/ The **Historical Association** are perhaps the premiere source of supporting the teaching and learning of history in this country. They have comprehensive materials for both teachers and pupils, covering the breadth of the curriculum. An excellent resource for all stakeholders.
ICT	http://www.teach-ict.com/index.html **Teach ICT** is a website with a host of resources for pupils in Key Stage 3 to 5.
	https://getkahoot.com **Kahoot** is a game-based learning with so much more than just a quiz format. It challenges pupils and raises the bar for progress and achievement indicators.
Maths	https://hegartymaths.com/ **Hegarty Maths'** aim is to help pupils who need a little extra support in math and provides them with a platform to work hard and access to the opportunities and choices to be successful in their lives.
	https://www.mymaths.co.uk/ **MyMaths** provides complete curriculum coverage for teachers from Key Stage 1 to A Level, MyMaths offers a wealth of resources that will help you deliver your teaching in the classroom and develop your pupils' confidence and fluency in math.
	https://justmaths.co.uk/ **Just Maths** provides GCSE Maths revision, resources and tutorials for teachers and students.
	https://www.onmaths.com/ **On Maths** is a treasure trove of examination preparation materials for pupils.

MFL	https://languagesonline.org.uk/Hotpotatoes/index.html **Languages online** has loads of resources for teachers and pupils in a number of languages for all year groups.
	https://www.memrise.com/ **Memrise** offers thousands of video clips to help pupils learn and memorise MFL.
	https://schools.duolingo.com/ **Duo lingo** is a site for MFL teachers, advertising itself as the most popular language learning platform for schools.
Music	https://www.mfy.org.uk/about/education/classroom/ **Music for Youth** is a tried and tested resource bank and has free resources for teachers.
	https://www.rhinegold.co.uk/wp-content/uploads/2015/10/MT0518-scheme-KS3-4-5-Free-online-resources.pdf **Rhinegold** lists loads of free online resources for music teachers
PE	https://www.youtube.com/channel/UC4aEFy_BrFnHC3S-x1Bsfqw Youtube.com - **MR BTEC** - Everything a pupil needs to know to pass BTEC Sport.
	https://www.peresourcesbank.co.uk/ PE **Resources Bank** has a wealth of practice exam questions for pupils and teachers of GCSE PE.
	Https://Primarypeplanning.Com/ *Primary PE Planning - the UK's fastest growing provider of online PE lesson planning resources for teachers.*
PSHE	https://www.pshe-association.org.uk/curriculum-and-resources/resources/rise-above-schools-teaching-resources The **PSHE Association** offers teachers free PSHE resources from Public Health England on health, wellbeing and resilience.
	https://www.schoolwellbeing.co.uk/resources?theme=10 **School wellbeing** offers many resources for teachers and are free to download.
RE	https://www.natre.org.uk/resources/ **National Association of Teachers of Religious Education** is a website for teachers with loads of resources, advice and guidance.
	https://www.reonline.org.uk/ **RE Online** – free resources for teachers that are of a high quality.
	truetube.co.uk **True Tube** offers award winning free resources for teachers for RE, PSHE and Citizenship.

	theresite.org.uk **The RE site** is Religious Education on the web offering practical ideas, resources and inspiration for teachers.
	request.org.uk **RE Quest** is a useful support site for teachers looking for current, up-to-date resources.
Science	https://www.senecalearning.com/ **Seneca Learning** is an independent learning resource for pupils with scripted information on which pupils can then test themselves, including practice with the long 4-mark and 6-mark questions.
	https://www.freesciencelessons.co.uk/ **Free Science Lessons** is a useful site for teachers and pupils supporting exam preparation.

Suggested books

▦ **Educational Inspection Framework: Overview of the research.**

Ofsted, 2019a.

A comprehensive and up-to-date resume of the current research behind Ofsted's 2019 framework.

▦ **Embedded Formative Assessment (Second edition).**

Dylan Wiliam, 2018.

A wealth of classroom strategies for classroom assessment the helps drive pupil engagement and learning.

▦ **Mindset: Changing the way you think to fulfil your potential**

Carol S. Dweck, 2017.

An updated version of this hugely influential work.

▦ **Much Promise: Successful Schools in England**

Barnaby Lenon, 2017.

The first half of the book offers a review of current research about what we do (and do not do) in schools that affect our most vulnerable pupils. The second half of the book offers us several case studies schools where we can see best practice in action.

▦ **Making Good Progress? The Future of Assessment for Learning**

Daisy Christodoulou, 2016.

Making Good Progress? outlines practical recommendations and support that Primary and Secondary teachers can follow in order to achieve the most effective classroom-based approach to ongoing assessment.

The School Leadership Journey

John Dunford, 2016.

A good overview of education at a local and national level from an author who has been at the top of education in the UK for many years.

Headstrong: 11 Lessons of School Leadership

Dame Sally Coates, 2015.

Personal journey of an outstanding headteacher, her experiences in leadership and the 11 lessons she implemented to great success, that any school leader may benefit from also learning.

Designing group work: strategies for heterogeneous classrooms

Elizabeth Cohen and Rachel Lotan, 2014.

A wonderful go-to compendium of information on all things related to group work. If you spend most of your lessons teaching groups – this book is a treasure trove of information for you.

A Taxonomy for Learning, Teaching and Assessing: A Revision of Bloom's Taxonomy

Anderson and Krathwohl, 2013.

If you have never read in detail one of the foundation stones of contemporary education, here is an updated version.

Visible Learning: A synthesis of meta-analysis relating to achievement.

John Hattie, 2009.

More than fifteen years' research into what makes effective teaching is encapsulated in this seminal work.

How We Learn. Learning and non-learning in school and beyond.

Knud Illeris, 2007.

A masterpiece in really looking at how we learn and how learning and non-learning take place.

Bibliography

Aaronson, D., Barrow, L. and Sander, W. (2007). Teachers and pupil achievement in the Chicago public high schools, in *Journal of Labor Economics*, 25(1) 95–135.

Allen, R., Jerrim, J., Paraweshwaram, M. and Thomson, D. (2018). *Properties of Commercial Tests in the EEF Database*. London: EEF.

Anderson, L.W. and Krathwohl, D.R. (2001). *A Taxonomy for Learning, Teaching, and Assessing: A Revision of Bloom's Taxonomy of Educational Objectives*. London: Pearson.

Askew, M. and Wiliam, D. (1995). *Recent Research in Mathematics Education 5–16: Ofsted Reviews of Research*. London: HMSO.

Barenberg, J., Roeder, U.R. and Dutke, S. (2018). Pupils' temporal distributing of learning activities in psychology courses: Factors of influence and effects on the metacognitive learning outcome, in *Psychology Learning and Teaching*, 17(3) 257–271.

Bennett, R.E. (2011). Formative assessment: A critical review, in *Assessment in Education: Principles, Policy and Practice*, 18(1) 5–25.

Biesta, G. (2008). Good education in an age of measurement: On the need to reconnect with the question of purpose in education, in *Educational Assessment, Evaluation and Accountability*, 21(1) 33–46.

Birbalsingh, K. (2016). *Battle Hymn of the Tiger Teachers*. Woodbridge: John Catt.

Brophy, J. and Good, T.L. (1986). Teacher behavior and pupil achievement in M.C. Wittrock (Ed) *Handbook of Research on Teaching (3rd edition)*. New York: MacMillan.

Capar, G. and Tarim, K. (2015). Efficacy of the cooperative learning method on mathematics achievement and attitude: A meta-analysis research, in *Educational Sciences: Theory and Practice*, 15(2) 553–559.

Chmitorz, A., Kunzler, A., Helmreich, I., Tüscher, O., Kalisch, R., Kubiak, T., Wessa, M. and Lieb, K. (2018). Intervention studies to foster resilience – A systematic review and proposal for a resilience framework in future intervention studies, in *Clinical Psychology Review*, 59 78–100.

Christodoulou, D. (2016). *Making Good Progress: The Future of Assessment for Learning*. Oxford: Oxford University Press.

Clark, J.M. and Paivio, A. (1991). Dual coding theory and education, in *Educational Psychology Review*, 3, 149–210.

Coates, S. (2015). *Head Strong: 11 Lessons in School Leadership*. Woodbridge, ON: John Catt.

Coe, R., Aloisi, C., Higgins, S. and Elliot Major, L. (2014). *What Makes Great Teaching? Review of the Underpinning Research.* Sutton Trust.

Cohen, E. and Lotan, R. (2014). *Designing Group Work: Strategies for Heterogeneous Classrooms.* New York: Teachers College Press.

Cooper Gibson Research (2017). *Understanding Schools' Responses to the Progress 8 Accountability Measure.* Department for Education: London.

Cordingley, P., Higgins, S., Greany, T., Buckler, N., Coles-Jordan, D., Crisp, B., Saunders, L. and Coe, R. (2015). *Developing Great Teaching: Lessons from the International Reviews into Effective Professional Development.* London: Teacher Development Trust.

Creemers, B. (1994). *The Effective Classroom.* London: Cassell.

Creemers, B. and Kyriakides, L. (2008). *The Dynamics of Educational Effectiveness: A Contribution to Policy, Practice and Theory in Contemporary Schools.* London: Routledge.

Curry, L. (1990). *Learning Styles in Secondary Schools: A Review of Instruments and Implications for Their Use* (Thesis). Madison,WI: University of Wisconsin.

Dann, R. (2016). Understanding and enhancing pupils' learning progress in schools in deprived communities, in *Education 3–13*, 44(1) 19–31.

DfE (2011). *Teachers' Standards.* London: DfE.

DfE (2015). *Final Report of the Commission on Assessment Without Levels.* London: DfE.

DfE (2016). *Progress 8 Measure in 2016, 2017, and 2018 Guide for Maintained Secondary Schools, Academies and Free Schools.* London: DfE.

DfE (2018). *Schools, Pupils and their Characteristics: January 2018.* London: DfE.

DfE (2019). *Pupil Absence in Schools in England, Autumn term 2018.* London: DfE.

DfEE (2001). *Statistics of Education. Pupil Progress in Schools in England, 2000.* London. DfEE.

Deunk, M.I., Smale-Jacobse, A.E., de Boer, H., Doolaardand, S. and Bosker, R.J. (2015). Effective differentiation practices: A systematic review and meta-analysis of studies on the cognitive effects of differentiation practices in primary education in *Educational Research Review*, 24(1) 31–54.

Dewey, J. (1897). My pedagogic creed, in *School Journal*, 54(3) 77–80.

Dudek, C.M., Reddy, L.A., Lekwa, A., Hua, A.N., and Fabiano, G.A. (2019). Improving universal classroom practices through teacher formative assessment and coaching, in *Assessment for Effective Intervention*, 44(2) 81–94.

Dunford, J. (2016). *The School Leadership Journey.* Woodbridge: John Catt.

Dunlowsky, J., Rawson, K.A., Marsh, E.J., Nathan, M.J., and Willingham, D.T. (2013). Improving pupils' learning with effective learning techniques promising directions from cognitive and educational psychology, in *Psychological Science in the Public Interest*, 14(1) 4–58.

Dyer, O. (2016). Drill and Didactic Teaching Work Best, in *Battle Hymn of the Tiger Teachers* (K. Birbalsingh, Ed.). Woodbridge: John Catt.

Ehren, M., Gustafsson, J., Altrichter, H., Skedsmo, G., Kemethofer, D. and Huber, S. (2015), Comparing effects and side effects of different school inspection systems across Europe, in *Comparative Education*, 51(3) 205, 375–400.

Elliott, V., Baird, J., Hopfenbeck, T.N., Ingram, J., Thompson, J., Usher, N. and Zantout, M. (2016). *A Marked Improvement? A Review of the Evidence on Written Marking.* London: EEF.

Fielding, M. and Moss, P. (2011). *Radical Education and the Common School: A Democratic Alternative.* London: Routledge.

Galton, M. and Simon, B. (1980). *Progress and Performance in the Primary Classroom.* London: Routledge.

Gardner, H. (1993). *Frames of Mind.* London: Fontana.

Gill, T. (2017). *The impact of the Introduction of Progress 8 on the Uptake and Provision of Qualifications in English schools.* Cambridge: Cambridge University.

Halverson, R. and Smith, A. (2009). How new technologies have (and have not) changed teaching and learning in schools, *Journal of Computing in Teacher Education*, 26(2) 49–54.

Hamre, B.K. and Pianta, R.C. (2005). Can instructional and emotional support in the first-grade classroom make a difference for children at risk of school failure? *Child Development*, 76, 949–967.

Hanson, T.E., Austin, G. and Lee-Bayha, J. (2004). *Ensuring that No Child is Left Behind: How Are Pupil Health Risks & Resilience Related to the Academic Progress of Schools?* San Francisco, CA: WestEd.

Hanuskek, E.A. and Rivkin, S.G. (2006). Teacher Quality in *Handbook of the Economics of Education*, Volume 2, University of Texas, TX: Dallas.

Hargreaves, E. (2005). Assessment for learning? Thinking outside the (black) box, *Cambridge Journal of Education*, 35(2) 213–224.

Harlen, W. (2003). *A Systematic Review of the Evidence of Reliability and Validity of Assessment By Teachers Used for Summative Purposes.* London: Institute of Education.

Hattie, J. (2009). *Visible Learning: A Synthesis of Meta-analysis Relating to Achievement.* New York: Routledge.

Hattie, J. (2012). *Visible Learning for Teachers: Maximising Impact on Learning.* London: Routledge.

Hattie J (2015) *What Works Best in Education: The Politics of Collaborative Expertise.* London: Pearson.

Higton, J., Leonardi, S., Richards, N., Choudoury, A., Sofroniou, N. and Owen, D. (2017). *Teacher Workload Survey, 2016.* London: Department for Education.

Holcomb, P.J., Kounios, J., Anderson, J.E., and West, W.C. (1999). Dual coding, context availability, and concreteness effects in sentence comprehension: An electrophysiological investigation, in *Journal of Experimental Psychology: Learning, Memory, and Cognition*, 25, 721–742.

Hood, M. (2016). *Beyond the Plateau.* London: IPPR.

Hunt, E. and Vernoit, J. (2014). *Valuing Educational Progress in England: The Economic Benefits of the Progress Made in GCSE Performance.* London: Department for Education.

Illeris, K. (2007). *How We Learn. Learning and Non-learning in School and Beyond.* London: Routledge.

Jahan, M. (2010). *Educational Influences on Pupil Academic Attainment: A Multi-level Analysis in the Context of Bangladesh* (Thesis). Nottingham: University of Nottingham.

Jones, K., Tymms, P., Kemethofer, D., O'Hara, J., McNamara, G., Huber, S., Myrberg, E., Skedsmo, G. and Greger, D. (2017). The unintended consequences of school inspection: The prevalence of inspection side-effects in Austria, the Czech Republic, England, Ireland, the Netherlands, Sweden, and Switzerland', in *Oxford Review of Education*, 43(6) 805–822.

Kane, T.J. and Cantrell, S. (2010). *Learning About Teaching Initial Findings from the Measures of Effective Teaching Project.* New York: The Bill and Melinda Gates Foundation.

Kelly, A. and Downey, C. (2011). *Using Effectiveness Data for School Improvement: Developing and utilising Metrics*. London: Routledge.

Kirby, J. (2016). Knowledge, memory and testing, in *Battle Hymn of the Tiger Teachers, in* K. Birbalsingh (Ed). Woodbridge: John Catt.

Kirschner, P.A. (2002). Cognitive load theory: Implications of cognitive load theory on the design of learning, in *Learning and Instruction*, 12(1) 1–10.

Kirschner, P.A., Sweller, J. and Clark, R.E. (2006). Why minimal guidance during instruction does not work: An analysis of the failure of constructivist, discovery, problem-based, experiential, and inquiry-based Teaching, in *Educational Psychologist*, 41(2) 75–86.

Kirschner, P.A., Sweller, J., Kirschner, F. and Zambrano, J. (2018). From cognitive load theory to collaborative cognitive load theory, in *International Journal of Computer-Supported Collaborative Learning*, 13(2) 213–233.

Knight, B.A. (2015). *Teachers' Use of Textbooks in the Digital Age*. London: Cogent.

Kriegbaum, K., Becker, N. and Spinath, B. (2018). The Relative Importance of Intelligence and Motivation as Predictors of School Achievement: A meta-analysis, in *Educational Research Review*, 25(2) 120–148.

Kutnick, P and Blatchford, P. (2014). *Effective Group Work in Primary School Classrooms*, New York: Springer.

Kyriakides, L. and Creemers, B. (2008). A longitudinal study on the stability over time of school and teacher effects on pupil outcomes, in *Oxford Review of Education,* 34(5) 521–545.

Lane, P. (2019). Spark Video Strikes Back: Reigniting Learning and Practice in Presentations in a PowerPoint Dominated Universe, in *CELE Journal*, 27(1) 76–105.

Lenon, B. (2017). *Much Promise: Successful Schools in England*. Woodbridge: John Catt.

Lindvall, C.M. and Nitko, A.J. (1975). *Measuring Pupil Achievement and Aptitude*. New York: Harcourt, Brace and Javanovich.

Lyon, R.G. (1998). *The NICHD Research Program in Reading Development, Reading Disorders and Reading Instruction: A Summary. of Research Findings. Keys to Successful Learning: A National Summit on Research in Learning Disabilities*. New York: National Center for Learning Disabilities.

MacCallum, B. (2000). *Formative Assessment: Implications for Classroom Practice*. London: Institute of Education.

Mayer, R.E. and Moreno, R. (1998). A split-attention effect in multimedia learning: Evidence for dual processing systems in working memory, in *Journal of Educational Psychology*, 90, 312–320.

McCluskey, G. (2017). Mapping, measuring and monitoring achievement: Can a new evaluation framework help schools challenge inequalities? in *Improving Schools,* 20(1) 5–17.

Morris, T.T., Davies, N.M., Dorling, D., Richmond, R.C. and Smith, G.D. (2018). Testing the validity of value-added measures of educational progress with genetic data. *British Educational Research Journal,* 44(5) 725–747.

Muijs, D. and Reynolds, D. (2003). Pupil background and teacher effects on achievement and attainment in mathematics: A longitudinal study, in *Educational Research and Evaluation*, 9(3) 289–314.

Muijs, D. and Reynolds, D. (2017). *Effective Teaching, Evidence and Practice (4th edition)*. London: Sage.

Muijs, D., Kyriakides, L., van der Werf, G., Creemers, B., Timperley, H. and Earl, L. (2014). State of the Art – Teacher effectiveness and professional learning, in *School Effectiveness and School Improvement*, 25(2) 231–256.

Nasen (2014). *Tracking Progress and Managing Provision*. Tamworth, Staffordshire: Nasen.

OECD (2016). *Programme for International Pupil Assessment Results from PISA 2015*. Paris: OECD Publishing.

Offenberg, R.M. (2004). Inferring adequate yearly progress of schools from pupil achievement in highly mobile communities, in *Journal of Education for Pupils Placed at Risk*, 9(4) 337–355.

Ofsted (2003). *Good Assessment in Secondary Schools*. London: Ofsted.

Ofsted (2017). *Reception Curriculum in Good and Outstanding Primary Schools: Bold Beginnings*. London: Ofsted.

Ofsted (2019a). *Educational Inspection Framework: Overview of the Research*. London: Ofsted.

Ofsted (2019b). *The School Inspection Handbook*. London: Ofsted.

Paas, F., Renkl, A. and Sweller, J. (2003). Cognitive load theory and instructional design: Recent developments, in *Educational Psychologist,* 38, 1–4.

Pashler, H., Mcdaniel M., Rohrer, D. and Bjork, R. (2008). Learning styles: Concepts and evidence, in *Psychological Science in the Public Interest*, 9(3) 105–119.

Paterson, C. (2013). *Measuring What Matters: Secondary School Accountability Indicators that Benefit All*. London: Centre Forum and Pearson.

Peček, M., Zuljan, M.V., Čuk, I. and Lesar, I. (2008). Should assessment reflect only pupils' knowledge? in *Educational Studies*, 34(2) 73–82.

PSHE Association (2017). *PSHE Education - Programme of Study Key Stages 1–5*. London: PSHE Association.

Paivio, A. (1990). *Mental Representations: A Dual Coding Approach*. New York: Oxford University Press.

Polesel, J., Rice, S. and Dulfer, N. (2014). The impact of high-stakes testing on curriculum and pedagogy: a teacher perspective from Australia, in *Journal of Education Policy*, 29(5) 640–657.

Quigley, A.J. (2016). *The Confident Teacher*. London: Routledge.

Rawson, K.A. and Kintsch, W. (2005). Rereading effects depend on time of test, in *Journal of Educational Psychology*, 97(1) 70–80.

Reynolds, D., Sammons, S., De Fraine, B., Van Damme, J., Townsend, T., Teddlie, C. and Stringfield, S. (2014). Educational effectiveness research (EER): A state-of-the-art review, in *School Effectiveness and School Improvement*, 25(2) 197–230.

Richland, L.E., Bjork, R.A., Finley, J.R. and Linn, J.C. (2005). Linking cognitive science to education: generation and interleaving effects in B.G. Bara, L. Barsalou and M. Bucciarelli (Eds) *Proceedings of the Twenty-Seventh Annual Conference of the Cognitive Science Society*, Mahwah, NJ: Lawrence Erlbaum.

Riener, C. and Willingham, D.T. (2010). The myth of learning styles, in *Change*, 42(5) 32–35.

Rohrer, D., and Taylor, K. (2006). The effects of overlearning and distributed practice on the retention of mathematics knowledge, in *Applied Cognitive Psychology*, 20, 1209–1224.

Rohrer, D. (2012). Interleaving helps pupils distinguish among similar concepts, in *Educational Psychology Review*, 24, 355–367.

Rohrer, D., Dedrick, R. and Stershic, S. (2014). Interleaved practice improves mathematics learning, in *Journal of Educational Psychology*, 107(3) 900–908.

Rook, C., Smith, L., Johnstone, J., Rossato, Lopez-Sanches, G., Suarez, A. and Roberts, J. (2018). Reconceptualising workplace resilience – a cross-disciplinary perspective, in *Anales de Psycologia*, 34(2) 332–339.

Rosenshine, B. and Stevens, R. (1986). Teaching functions in M.C. Wittrock (Ed), *Handbook of Research on Teaching* (3rd edition). New York: Macmillan.

Satterly, D. (1989). *Assessment in Schools (second edition)*. Oxford: Blackwell.

Scheerens, J. and Bosker, R. (1997). *The Foundations of Educational Effectiveness*, Oxford: Pergamon.

Silva, E. (2008). *Measuring Skills for the 21st Century*. Washington DC: Education Sector.

Slater, H., Davies, N and Burgess, S. (2009). *Do Teachers Matter? Measuring the Variation in teacher effectiveness in England*. London: Centre for Market and Public Organisation Working Series.

Smith, F., Hardman, F., Wall, K. and Mroz, M. (2004). Interactive whole class teaching in the National Numeracy and Literacy Strategies, in *British Educational Research Journal*, 30(3) 395–411.

Smith, L. and Land, M. (1981). Low-inference verbal behaviors related to teacher clarity, in *Journal of Classroom Interaction*, 17, 37–42.

Solomon, Y. and Lewin, C. (2016). Measuring 'progress': Performativity as both driver and constraint in school innovation, in *Journal of Education Policy*, 31(2) 226–238.

Sparks, R., Patton, J. and Murdoch, A. (2014). Early reading success and its relationship to reading achievement and reading volume: Replication of "10 years later", in *Reading and Writing*, 27(1) 189–211.

Stallings, J. (1985). Effective elementary classroom practices, in M.J Kyle (Ed), in *Reaching for Excellence: An Effective Sourcebook*, Washington, DC: US Governing Printing Office.

Steedman, J. (1980). *Progress in Secondary Schools*. London: NCB.

Stigler, J. and Hiebert, J. (1999). *The Teaching Gap: Best Ideas from the World's Teachers for Improving Education in the Classroom*. New York, NY: The Free Press.

Sutton Trust (2015). *Developing Teachers Improving Professional Development for Teachers*. London: Sutton Trust.

Swann, K. (1988). *How Can Classroom Practice Be Improved? An Investigation of the Logic of Learning in Classroom Practice* (Thesis). London: University of the South Bank.

Swann, M., Peacock, A., Drummond, M.J. and Hart, S. (2012). *Creating Learning Without Limits*. Milton Keynes: Open University Press.

Sweller, J. (2011). Cognitive load theory, in *Psychology of Learning and Motivation*, 55, 37–76.

Tomsett, J. (2015). *This Much I Know about Love and Fear....* Carmarthen: Crown.

Tough, P. (2012). *How Children Succeed: Grit, Curiosity, and the Hidden Power of Character*. Boston, MA: Houghton Mifflin Harcourt.

Turnbull, A.P. (2013). *Exceptional Lives: Special Education in Today's Schools*. London: Pearson.

UKCES (2014). *The Future of Work Jobs and Skills in 2030*. London: UKCES.

Van de Grift, W. (2009). Reliability and validity in measuring the value added of schools, in *School Effectiveness and School Improvement*, 20(2) 269–285.

Walberg, H.J. (1986). Syntheses of research on teaching, in M.C. Wittrock (Ed), in *Handbook of Research on Teaching, 3rd edition*. New York: Macmillan.

Welsh office, (1983). *Assessment and Monitoring of Progress in Secondary Schools*. Cardiff: Welsh Office.

Wiliam, D. (2011). *Teacher Quality: What It Is, Why It Matters and How to Get More of It*. London: Institute of Education.

Wiliam, D. (2018). *Embedded Formative Assessment (second edition)*. Bloomington, IN: Solution Tree Press.

Willingham, D.T. (2008). When and how neuroscience applies to education, in *Phi Delta Kappa*, 89(6) 421–423.

Windle, G. (2011). What is resilience? A review and concept analysis, in *Review in Clinical Gerontology*, 21 152–169.

Articles and Presentations

Allen, R. (2018). *What if we cannot measure pupil progress?* Accessible from: https://rebeccaallen.co.uk/2018/05/23/what-if-we-cannot-measure-pupil-progress/

Andrews, J. (2017). *The introduction of progress 8*. London: Education Policy Institute. Accessible from: https://epi.org.uk/publications-and-research/analysis-introduction-progress-8/

Benyohai, M. (2018). *The difference between measuring progress and attainment*. Accessible from: https://medium.com/@mrbenyohai/the-difference-between-measuring-progress-and-attainment-7269a41cdd8

Education Endowment Foundation (2019a). *Toolkit: Assessing monitoring pupil progress*. London: Education Endowment Foundation. Accessible from: https://educationendowmentfoundation.org.uk/tools/assessing-and-monitoring-pupil-progress/ampp-introduction/#closeSignup

Education Endowment Foundation (2019b). *Toolkit: Homework*. London: Education Endowment Foundation. Accessible from: https://educationendowmentfoundation.org.uk/evidence-summaries/teaching-learning-toolkit/homework-secondary/

Education Endowment Foundation (2019c). *Toolkit: Individualised instruction*. London: Education Endowment Foundation. Accessible from: https://educationendowmentfoundation.org.uk/evidence-summaries/teachinglearning-toolkit/individualised-instruction/.

Education Endowment Foundationi (2019d). *Improving outcomes for pupil premium pupils: metacognition and self-regulation*. Accessible from: https://educationendowmentfoundation.org.uk/evidence-summaries/teaching-learning-toolkit/meta-cognition-and-self-regulation/

Enser, M. (2019). *Why every teacher should be using dual coding*. Accessible from: https://www.tes.com/news/why-every-teacher-should-be-using-dual-coding

Lyon, G.R. (1999). *The NICHD research program in reading development, reading disorders and reading instruction*. NICHD: Keys to successful learning summit. Accessible from: https://eric.ed.gov/?id=ED430366.

Rosenshine, B. (1997). *The case for explicit, teacher-led, cognitive strategy instruction*, paper presented at the annual meeting of the American Educational Research Association, Chicago, IL. Accessible from: http://www.formapex.com/barak-rosenshine/616-the-case-for-explicit-teacher-led-cognitive-strategy-instruction?616d13afc6835dd26137b409becc9f87=339a5e-c40f56987efa4d7f134adb6e31

Serensen, B.M. (2017). *Let's ban powerpoint in lectures, it makes pupils more stupid and professors more boring.* Accessible from: https://www.independent.co.uk/news/education/lets-ban-powerpoint-in-lectures-it-makes-pupils-more-stupid-and-professors-more-boring-a7597506.html

Sharma, N. (2016). *Pupil mobility: What does it cost london?* London: London Councils. Accessible from: https://www.londoncouncils.gov.uk/node/29036

Sherrington, T. (2018). *Post: How can we measure and report progress meaningfully? Accessible from: https://teacherhead.com/2018/06/18/how-can-we-measure-and-report-progress-meaningfully/*

Third Space Learning (2019). *Debunking the myth of expected progress in KS1 and KS2: Life after levels in my primary school.* Accessible from: https://thirdspacelearning.com/blog/expected-progress-ks1-ks2-life-levels-primary-school/

Index

Note: *Italic* page numbers refer to figures.

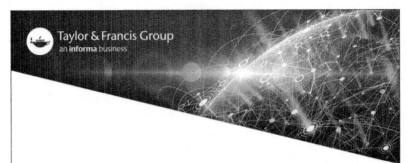

Taylor & Francis eBooks

www.taylorfrancis.com

A single destination for eBooks from Taylor & Francis
with increased functionality and an improved user
experience to meet the needs of our customers.

90,000+ eBooks of award-winning academic content in
Humanities, Social Science, Science, Technology, Engineering,
and Medical written by a global network of editors and authors.

TAYLOR & FRANCIS EBOOKS OFFERS:

A streamlined
experience for
our library
customers

A single point
of discovery
for all of our
eBook content

Improved
search and
discovery of
content at both
book and
chapter level

REQUEST A FREE TRIAL
support@taylorfrancis.com